THE U.S. CONSTITUTION AND CONSTITUTIONALISM IN AFRICA

Edited by

Kenneth W. Thompson

Volume V

In the Miller Center Bicentennial Series on Constitutionalism

UNIVERSITY PRESS OF AMERICA

Lanham • New York • London

The Miller Center

University of Virginia

University Press of America®, Inc.
4720 Boston Way
Lanham, Maryland 20706

3 Henrietta Street
London WC2E 8LU England

Printed in the United States of America
British Cataloging in Publication Information Available

Co-published by arrangement with
The White Burkett Miller Center of Public Affairs,
University of Virginia

Library of Congress Cataloging-in-Publication Data

The U.S. Constitution and constitutionalism in Africa /
edited by Kenneth W. Thompson.
p. cm. — (Miller Center bicentennial series on
constitutionalism ; v. 5)
1. Africa—Constitutional law. 2. United States—Constititional
law. I. Thompson, Kenneth W., 1921– . II. Series.
KF4554.U196 1989 342.73'02—dc20 89–24758 CIP
[347.3022]

ISBN 0–8191–7630–3 (alk. paper)
ISBN 0–8191–7631–1 (pbk. : alk. paper)

The paper used in this publication meets the minimum requirements of American National Standard for Information Sciences—Permanence of Paper for Printed Library Materials, ANSI Z39.48–1984.

Dedicated

to

all those who gave support to

the American effort to be

helpful

in

Africa

and to Africa's future

educators, philosophers and statesmen

Table of Contents

Preface

It is fitting that African constitutionalism be the focus of the fifth volume in the Miller Center Bicentennial Series. More perhaps than any other world region, Africa is a living laboratory for observing the interrelation between American, European and African ideas of constitutionalism. In some instances, American influence has been mediated through colonial governments who taught what Professor Mazrui has called "imperial history." Part of that "imperial history" included the struggle of the thirteen colonies to gain their independence from Britain. In other instances, the connection has been direct.

The influence of the United States on Africa is bound up with colonialism. When the United States sought "to help" Africa immediately following World War II, it did so in a strong spirit of anticolonialism. Americans sought to bring freedom and self-determination to Africa in what we considered a correction of the policies of the European colonial powers. The one exception, which prevented Americans from claiming to be wholly anticolonial, was our somewhat unhappy experience in Liberia. Elsewhere we saw our goals as convergent with those of Africans and therefore likely to contribute to their political and constitutional growth.

Africans saw us not only as anticolonial but domestically racist, as internationally espousing aims coinciding with theirs but domestically acting in ways antithetical to their values (*Plessy vs. Ferguson* maintained the principles of segregation). As we changed domestically with *Brown vs. the Board of Education*, we found ourselves almost overnight having become an imperial power. Thus, as Professor Mazrui argues, there were anomalies in the American position as viewed by Africans both early and later in the postwar period.

PREFACE

American constitutionalism had an influence both through our actions at different times in the postwar period and through the all too apparent gulf between our moral pronouncements and our behavior at home and abroad. One way or the other, we were destined to influence African developments, whether by example or by failure to practice what we had preached. In either case, Africa embraced ideas such as national self-determination and racial equality which Americans had professed and sometimes if not always practiced.

It is within this broader context that the contributors to this volume have approached constitutionalism. The liberal tradition has had a complicated, sometimes positive and other times negative interrelationship with African development. The subject is worthy of careful study and reflection and it is hoped the essays which follow will inspire that review. Thus while the focus of this volume is on constitutionalism, it is also on the forces and circumstances surrounding constitutionalism. In that sense, this is a book about "living constitutions," both written and unwritten.

Introduction

Exploring the influence of the American Constitution in Africa calls for a broader perspective than a study of the influence of constitutionalism in Asia—the subject of the preceding volume in this series. One reason is that American involvement in Africa has had a shorter time span. The story is relatively brief and is still unfolding. Another reason is, as Professor Mazrui points out, that a balance sheet must record that contradictions and ambiguities that are part of the history. Further, American influence has found its way into Africa along routes that are both direct and indirect. Our influence has found its way into Africa through American teachers, scientists, and consultants or advisers, but also through British, French, and European programs and people. Finally, Africans trained in the United States have returned to their countries sometimes as enthusiasts and converts but at other times alienated from social patterns in America, but not from the underlying values against which they judge our society and their own.

Professor Ali Mazrui of the University of Michigan and Cornell provides the framework paper for thinking about African constitutionalism. Born in Mombasa, Kenya, he was the first African to become a full professor in an East African university at least in the humanities and social sciences. Possessing intellectual powers of the highest order, he gained widespread respect, first at Makerere College in Kampala, Uganda and thereafter in the international community of scholars. Fearless in studying and identifying the main characteristics of both his native and adopted societies, he has earned the applause and sometimes the criticism of persons in both worlds. In reading his always penetrating and sometimes controversial interpretations, readers should try to join him in the search for truth rather than indulging themselves the satisfaction of premature judgments on his conclusions. They should seek with him to put themselves in African shoes so they may understand the forces at work in another culture.

Dr. Ibrahim A. Gambari is a former foreign minister of Nigeria and a prominent authority on political science in Nigeria and the United States. His major scholarly and research interest has been foreign policy but he is also completing a book on constitutionalism in Africa. He has taught at Ahmadu Bello University in Northern Nigeria and served as the director of the Institute of International Relations in Nigeria. In his discussion, Dr. Gambari analyzes the legitimacy of African governments and in particular military regimes in Africa. He looks at the prospects for democratic reform and the secular state in Africa and his warnings regarding threats to the latter are even more sobering than Professor Mazrui's interpretations. Whereas Mazrui sees the likelihood of an identification of ethnic and tribal groups with parties as being virtually inevitable necessitating one party rule temporarily, Gambari seems to put the prospects for political parties in another and more American perspective, holding out the prospect for two-party governments.

Islamic societies constitute an important segment of African political and legal systems and the rise of Islamic fundamentalism is a conspicuous development on the African scene. Therefore, any serious and inclusive discussion of African constitutionalism must take Islam into account.

Professor Abdullah an-Na'im is a highly respected Sudanese legal scholar who received his early training at the University of Khartoum and graduate training at Cambridge University in England and the University of Edinburgh. Having concentrated on criminal law procedures, he is uniquely qualified to discuss *Shari'a* and the draconian measures associated with it. He demonstrates, however, that except for certain hardline Islamic states such as Khomeini's Iran, *Shari'a* has been honored more in the breach. He discusses the place of human rights and public accountability in the Islamic state while also making clear Islam's outright rejection of any idea of the secular state.

Gambia offers a case study for testing the influence of the American Constitution and its ideas of constitutionalism. Professor Sulayman S. Nyang, who is a University of

Virginia Ph.D. in government and foreign affairs, analyzes the movement toward democracy in his native country. He was accredited in the Gambian Foreign Service serving as head of chancery and deputy head of mission in Saudi Arabia. He is currently director of African Studies at Howard University. His major work bespeaks an ongoing intellectual interest: *Islam, Christianity and African Identity: History and Political Analysis in Contemporary Africa.* It is especially instructive to compare his views with those of Africanists who precede him in this volume. He deals directly with the impact of the American Constitution in shaping the Gambian approach to a Bill of Rights, representative government, a supreme leader chosen by popular vote and freedom of religion.

South Africa stands apart from the other countries of Africa although its economic importance for some of them is beyond dispute. Any contemporary constitutional influence of the United States and Britain must occur in an atmosphere of crisis and conflict. Sir Patrick Moberly has dedicated his life to the British Foreign Service having held posts in Baghdad and Dakar as well as being British ambassador to South Africa and Israel. More recently he did research at the Harvard Center for International Affairs. His discussion underscores the limitations on influence from abroad in situations such as that of South Africa. At the same time, Sir Patrick delineates certain areas in which he considers that America and Britain have a role to play. It is noteworthy that his proposals exclude sanctions about which he has serious doubts, as he does policies of divestment.

The concluding essay is by Crawford Young, who served as dean of social sciences at Lubumbashi University in Zaire from 1973-75 following a period of teaching at Makerere College from 1965-66. Young has also held high leadership positions at the University of Wisconsin, including associate dean of the graduate school. He puts forward the proposition that democracy is on the move and then examines the various forms it is taking in different African countries. The questions that arise concern leading African states that seem not to fit this pattern and whether democracy as a process of governance can be equated with constitutionalism. One question not explored is the relation between worsening economic conditions and the future of emerging democracies. If the present economic decline continues, how will national publics judge their democratic regimes and what will such judgments portend for the future of democracy in Africa? It is issues such as these that bring African constitutionalism into the present era.

The American Constitution and the Liberal Option in Africa: Myth and Reality*

ALI MAZRUI

NARRATOR: Professor Mazrui is professor of politics and African studies at the University of Michigan. He was born in Mombasa, Kenya; he received a B.A. with distinction from the University of Manchester in 1960, a Master's degree from Columbia, and a D.Phil. from Oxford. He spent nearly a decade teaching at that little gem of a university, Makerere University. First it was Makerere College and then Makerere University, a part of the University of East Africa. He started out as a lecturer, then became the first African professor. Later he became head of the department, and finally dean of the faculty at Makerere.

He came to the University of Michigan in 1974. (Maybe there wasn't room for Idi Amin and him in Uganda!) There he soon established himself as the leading scholar on African politics in this country. He is also professor in the Center for Afro-American and African studies at Michigan. Since 1986 he has also been Andrew D. White professor-at-large at Cornell University. (Being professor-at-large means you come when they call you, so in this connection he periodically takes part in programs at Cornell.) He also was research professor at the University of Jos in Nigeria until recently.

**Presented in a forum at the Miller Center on January 4, 1989.*

In 1979 he delivered the Reith Lectures for the BBC in London. He was author, narrator, and presenter of the program *The Africans: A Triple Heritage*, which was first produced by the BBC and WETA and then aired on PBS. He has been visiting professor at many universities both here in the United States and abroad; he is editor of Volume VIII of a general history series, *The UNESCO General History of Africa.* He has been the president of the American African Studies Association and also vice president and president of the International Congress of African Studies. He is the author of numerous works including *Towards a Pax Africana; A World Federation of Cultures*; and *Africa's International Relations.*

Professor Mazrui will speak to us in our series on constitutionalism, specifically on the comparative aspects of constitutionalism. His topic is "The American Constitution and the Liberal Option in Africa: Myth and Reality." It is a great pleasure to have you with us.

PROFESSOR MAZRUI: Thank you very much. I'm delighted to be here. It is a privilege to be at these distinguished institutions, both the University and the Center. I was delighted when my old friend, Ken Thompson, got in touch and asked me to come and share some thoughts with you about aspects of the African constitutional experience.

First, we ought to bear in mind that the diffusion of American constitutional ideas is inseparable from the spread of other aspects of American political culture. The spread of constitutional ideas emanating from this country are not neatly separable from the political ones, and the diffusion of American political ideas goes back to our colonial period in Africa. Some of it came, ironically, through colonial education, so, for example, British Africa introduced the young Africans to America through its imperial history, including the War of Independence. What we were learning, then, was "empire history," that is, the history of the British empire. That history included its hiccups, the biggest of which was the American War of Independence. That was featured in the days when I was in high school in Mombasa in Kenya. America became part of imperial history in that way.

In French Africa, America was part of the history of revolution because the French Revolution, whose two hundredth anniversary is being celebrated this year, was quite often presented in francophone colonial schools alongside revolutionary trends elsewhere. Of course this history emphasized, though, the uniqueness of the French experience. So even though the American experience took place earlier in history, it had to play second fiddle in the French schools to the basic innovativeness of the French experience. Nevertheless, Montesquieu and Tocqueville, as well as Rousseau, became introductions to America as well as introductions to the French experience.

In Anglophone Africa, that is in English-speaking Africa, students learned about both revolutions in classes about political philosophy. This was true especially in the early years after independence. Classes in political philosophy in African institutions could include Edmund Burke, who wrote of course an especially memorable piece on the French Revolution, but who was also concerned about the American experience with comparative revolution as a subfield.

John Locke, who influenced the American Revolution itself, was also featured as part of British political philosophy in schools, especially in the early post-colonial period. Locke, as you certainly know, contributed to Jefferson's phrase, "Life, liberty and the pursuit of happiness," in the Declaration of Independence. In fact Locke's formulation was "life, liberty and estate," but it may be that the pursuit of "estate" means the same thing as the pursuit of happiness to a property-owning democracy.

In short, we were introduced fairly early to these ideas, partly through colonial education. And then later on the diffusion of American constitutional and political culture came more directly through studying in the United States. In the interwar years, between the First World War and the Second World War, the United States was anticolonialist abroad and racist at home, and both factors were relevant. So Kwame Nkrumah, who later became president of Ghana, and Nnamdi Azikiwe, who later became president of Nigeria, were here in the United States when the legacy of *Plessy v. Ferguson* was still kicking. Moreover, the doctrine of separate but equal was alive and well, so they came before the changes which followed later in the century.

The impact of the U.S. Constitution is, then, not merely through its imitators and admirers; sometimes it has an impact through its detractors and critics. Rebelling *against* aspects of the U.S. Constitution was itself a form of impact. Nkrumah and Azikiwe were radicalized as students in the U.S.A., partly because the U.S. constitutional order was at that time racist. In fact, the United States was more racist than the Gold Coast from which Nkrumah had come. Paradoxically, England was at that time less racist at home than the Gold Coast that it had colonized. England was also less racist than the United States.

I certainly remember in my own experience, which was later than that of Nkrumah and Azikiwe, that I found an atmosphere of far less racism in Britain than in the colonial Kenya from which I came. (Even the idea of having my shoes polished by a white man in London was so mind-boggling that I got a friend to take photographs to send home.) On the other hand again, after Ken Thompson's efforts to get me to the United States, I did find that the United States, even as late as 1960, was a more racist society than Great Britain. For instance, for five years I had never been queried when I wanted a haircut at a barbershop in Britain. In my very first year (1960) in the United States, though, I went to a barbershop in Washington, D.C. and was refused a haircut on grounds connected with the exotic texture of my hair, in spite of my emphasis that I was prepared to take the risk.

The Rockefeller Foundation at the time was also worried about my movements. Again it is amazing that as late as 1960 the Rockefeller Foundation said that if I insisted on coming to the South, I should discuss the matter in detail with them in advance. They made it sound as if I was going to a war zone by coming to the South. Since this was in 1960, you can imagine the effect of American racism on Nkrumah twenty to thirty years earlier.

In short the United States had the virtue of anticolonialism abroad and the vice of racism at home. Both American racism and anticolonialism were radicalizing for younger Africans who later played such a decisive role in their own societies.

Then came the famous Supreme Court case, *Brown v. the Board of Education* [of Topeka, Kansas] and a new constitutional order, in terms of race, within the United States. At the same time the United States was consolidating itself as a superpower. What happened, then, was a kind of reversal of the old relationship between the American imperial role and the American racial role. Whereas the United States had once been anticolonial but racist, after World War II the United States became less racist at home and more imperialist abroad. So there was a kind of reversed emphasis in the impact of the United States on Africans. The U.S.A. claimed increasing privileges in intervening in the affairs of other nations; it took on a considerable imperial role, not of the old kind of claiming territory with a flag, but of wanting to control other societies. At the same time the United States also became less racially segregationist domestically. In sum, the diffusion of American constitutional ideas was affected by a new paradox which was emerging, a partial reversal of the old order of an anticolonial America that was at the same time domestically racist. Now more recently the diffusion of American constitutional ideas has come partly through this new American imperialism, which is a kind of cultural imperialism.

Africans have been inspired by contradictory aspects of American political and constitutional experience. Is it contradictory? An important part Jefferson has always symbolized in African political thought is a belief in national self-determination, partly because of his role in the American Declaration of Independence. Lincoln, on the other hand, has symbolized American *limits* to self-determination, so it is as if Jefferson proclaimed in favor of national self-determination, and Lincoln against regional self-determination. While Jefferson spoke *for* independence of the country, Lincoln aborted the southern bid for a separate identity.

Both of these lessons were embraced by Africa. There was a militant struggle for independence from colonial rule, but also an uncompromising hostility to regional or ethnic separatists. So both the Jeffersonian Declaration of Independence and Lincoln's "In Defense of the Union" have become part of African political predispositions since independence. For example, in Nigeria Azikiwe, who was educated here in part, quite often literally used Jeffersonian rhetoric and the language of Jeffersonian ideas. Then, after independence, Yakubu Gowon came to play the role of an antisecessionist Lincoln in Nigeria. He presided over the Nigerian civil war from 1967 to 1970, just as Lincoln had presided over the American Civil War some 100 years earlier. In fact Gowon had some of the same moral qualities that Americans, especially Americans in the North, often associate with Lincoln. Gowon made a transition, though, not from the log cabin to the White House, but, to the contrary, from the State House to the log cabin. He wasn't assassinated, but he was overthrown in a military coup in 1975.

He then became the only head of state of whom I know who fell from supreme power of a country as large as Nigeria to become a freshman undergraduate at a provincial British university. Literally a couple of years after he was being honored by Cambridge University in England as Nigeria's Head of State, he was standing in line in a college cafeteria at Warwick University as a freshman. He struggled for his Bachelor's degree and later worked his way to a well-earned Ph.D.; indeed, his was not the type of degree that heads of state normally have, which are honorary degrees, but an actual Ph.D. like the ones that you and I struggled for. So if Gowon was not Nigeria's Lincoln, then perhaps Lincoln was America's Gowon a hundred years in advance. Both saved their united governments successfully, and the U.S. experience helped to legitimize Africa's implacable opposition to secessionism. We can always point out that Americans had to do it at a high cost in human lives. Likewise we've had a series of civil wars to abort secessionism in Africa at a similarly high cost in human lives, but there is always the American precedent to lend Western legitimacy to what we are doing.

So applause for national independence and opposition to regional self-determination continues to be at the center of Africa's political ethos. The precedent was set by Jefferson, a symbol of independence, and by Lincoln, a symbol of national integrity.

Now this in turn is part of a wider dialectic in the American experience which is relevant to us, that is, the dialectic between a tendency for outer expansion and inner differentiation. To take up this first tendency, America has had a love affair with scale, which is part of its expansionist tendency, going back in its political manifestation to the manifest destiny of the 19th century and even earlier.

Likewise pan-Africanists—people who believe in African unity—have often been infatuated by territorial scale. They often quite consciously have the American precedent in mind, often forgetting that much of the land in America was obtained by imperialist means, either from Mexico after wars or bought from fellow imperialist states like France (Louisiana), or czarist Russia (Alaska). Nevertheless, the very largeness of the American political entity has been itself an important idea in African political thought. Nkrumah's admiration went further back to the original thirteen colonies and their decision to find a basis of unity in America. So pan-Africanism has often invoked the American precedent once again.

Then federalism emerged out of precisely the same concept of the thirteen colonies uniting to have government on a bigger scale. This federal principle, often consciously inspired by American experience, has been revised and redefined in a number of African countries.

Unfortunately federalism is not one of Africa's success stories. It has survived in Nigeria, though, after confronting the issue of how many states are viable in a federation. Nigeria, as you know, began by having units which were too large as states or regions. At independence there were three regions: north, east, and west; the creation of a fourth state, the midwest, was not enough to avert catastrophe. The First Republic of Nigeria, which basically lasted through the first half of the 1960s, was not a confederation of equally large and autonomous states; it was a federation in which one region or one state—the north—was so large that it virtually dominated the rest of the country. This was a prescription for disaster, and a civil war did ensue from 1967 to 1970.

Sudan, after the 1972 Addis Ababa Accords, also attempted a kind of federal status for the south. It was more like the kind of status given to northern Ireland in the United Kingdom roughly between the 1920s and 1960s, both experiments giving autonomy to one subsection of the country. Both the U.K.'s and Sudan's attempts—northern Ireland and southern Sudan—to achieve autonomous quasi-federal states, in fact failed. Religious differences were relevant in both failures, in both northern Ireland and southern Sudan.

In the case of Sudan, President Jaffer Nimeiri attempted to deal with the issue of too few states in the union. He announced the policy of redivision designed to create smaller states in the south and new states in the north. In a way it made sense. Unfortunately, his policy of redivision (a quasi-federal idea with units smaller than the north-south division that they had attempted), although politically rational in itself, came at a time when he also wanted to introduce Islamic law as state policy in the country. So while the redivision was rational, the introduction of Islamic law was regionally explosive in the south. The whole federal idea of redivision was consumed by Sudan's second civil war. As you know, the first one war took place between 1955 and 1972; then, in 1983, with the introduction of Islam as the basis of law, the second Sudanese civil war erupted and is still continuing to the present time.

Although we presented federalism as part of America's expansion, the expansionist credo of scale, federalism is also part of America's credo of differentiation. That is, when federalism unites people who would otherwise live in separate countries, it is an expansionist creed. On the other hand, when federalism concedes autonomy to provinces which would be otherwise dominated by the center, it is a creed of differentiation.

We can see such differentiation in Nigeria, for example. It entered the 1960s with three constituent states in its federation, as we said, but it entered the 1980s with nineteen. Clearly this meant greater differentiation. Many constituent states turned out to be more viable than the few states in keeping the federation together. The three were much more dangerous and fragile than the nineteen, strictly from the point of view of federalism.

Another area of differentiation is differentiation of church from state. Not many Africans are conscious of the fact that Americans virtually invented the secular state and virtually invented the idea of actual constitutional separation of church and state. In fact Africa's record on this score is mixed. We already mentioned that in the case of Sudan, Nimeiri abandoned the secular state and introduced the Islamic state in the 1980s.

On the other hand, Senegal's performance in the secular ethic is one area where Africa has done better than the United States in precisely a value shared with the United States. In other words, Senegal's performance in distilling the principle of church-state separation has been more successful than that of the United States. Separating church from state admittedly doesn't always lead to separating religion from politics, because separating church from state is very often a feasible institutional arrangement. Separating religion from politics, by contrast, means changing behavioral patterns, to have people behave in a way in which they regard religion as irrelevant to their political behavior.

It is useful to compare the model of John Kennedy with the model of Leopold Senghor in Senegal in this context. The result is a rather stark contrast. In 1960 the United States was trying to make up its mind whether to have a non-protestant as head of state for the first time. This was in a country which had had separation of church from state for nearly 200 years at that time, and yet it was still hesitating. To the end of our days we shall never know whether Kennedy was in fact elected. We only know that he became President. Though he *became* President, we don't know whether the hanky-panky in Illinois made enough of a difference so that in fact Nixon was denied a victory. (We'll never know because Nixon was advised not to challenge the election, and in the end he did not.) This was the first time that America looked outside of the Protestant fellowship for its President, and this was in a society which had institutionally and constitutionally separated church from state. Behaviorally, though, it had failed to separate religion from politics until that point.

I suspect the United States won't elect a person of Jewish faith to be head of state, certainly not in this century; it won't happen. The Jews that excel in other areas of American national life, of national endeavor, have themselves avoided bidding for the highest office in the land for very good pragmatic reasons. They are just terrified that this might let loose the demon of anti-semitism, that even attempting to attain the highest office might release the demon of anti-semitism in American society.

There are as many Muslims as Jews now in the United States. Therefore, a country which separates church from state should presumably make it conceivable for a Muslim to become president of the United States. I suspect that's not likely to happen, even in the next century, let alone this century. To have a Muslim president of the United States, however effectively church may be separated from state institutionally and constitutionally, is not likely to be achieved in the near future through the behavioral transformation of the American electorate.

Thus we should note that when your people were arguing in 1960 whether to choose a Christian, a fellow Christian of another persuasion to be head of state, the Senegalese, who are 80 percent Muslim, chose a Roman Catholic to be their head of state. That was Leopold Senghor. And it wasn't just a flash in the pan. Senghor worked out agreements with the Muslim leadership in the country. The society was ready to accept a Roman Catholic as its ultimate leader. He lasted as president nearly two decades in Senegal, a part of Africa that is relatively open and plural. Moreover, he was the first African ever to voluntarily step down from the post of head of state in postwar Africa, to just retire. The Senegalese voters were not just choosing another Muslim of a different denomination to become their leader; they were not a Christian electorate agonizing whether to have a Catholic Christian for head of state. The Senegalese were a Muslim electorate deciding to have a Roman Catholic president for their leader.

Likewise in Tanzania there is a Muslim plurality over the Christians, but Julius Nyerere, a Christian, was president of Tanzania from the time the country became independent in 1961 until he voluntarily stepped down in 1985. The fact that he belonged to a different religion was not a major issue in his credentials for office. People criticized Nyerere for a variety of other reasons, but the fact that he was a Roman Catholic was not one of them.

To return to the case of Senegal, now that Senghor has retired, there is a Muslim president for the first time since independence in this largely Muslim society. Just to emphasize how broad-minded the Senegalese continue to be, though, we could note that it wasn't a political handicap to this Muslim president that the first lady was a Roman Catholic. In fact, the First Lady of Senegal to the present day is a Roman Catholic.

On the issue of differentiation between church and state, a few Africans have abandoned the secular state. Most African countries have accepted it; it was virtually invented by the Americans. Independently of the American precedent, though, the Senegalese have performed better than the Americans themselves.

Politically, the most important areas of differentiation are capitalist differentiation and liberal democratic differentiation in the American constitutional and political experience. The separation of the state from the economy is the ideological foundation of American capitalism, a kind of economic pluralism. On the protection of the individual from the state, the foundation is American liberal democracy or political pluralism.

African capitalism was originally transmitted by Europe, and the European transmission of capitalism caused severe distortion in Africa. Basically until this last quarter of the twentieth century, the greatest enemy of capitalism in Africa has been the West. The West has made the chances of capitalism very fragile and frail, partly because the West brought it in as part of a larger colonial order. As a result the distrust of capitalism was tied in with the distrust of imperialism. The West created institutions as a colonial power which were statist and which therefore reduced the role of the private sector as understood by classical capitalism.

Moreover, the West was more interested in creating African wage labor than in creating African entrepreneurial skills. Therefore, there was a basic distortion all the time with one side of capitalism (that which could produce entrepreneurship) severely restricted or even aborted, and the other side (that needing labor) being developed and sometimes encouraged through a tax system. So taxes, which Americans rebelled against because they were not accompanied by representation, were used by Western colonial powers to persuade otherwise self-subsistent Africans to work for Europeans for wages. The Europeans had a wonderful system for extracting capital. They said, we'll charge you taxes, and you must pay them in money. We are printing the money, and so you have to make the money. You can get it by working for me; in short, I'll pay you with the money *I* have printed so that you can cultivate *your* land for *my* benefits. Thus, the conditions for proletarianization were created, but not conditions for the emergence of an entrepreneurial middle class.

The result of this was that Western tastes without Western skills became part of the African condition; Western consumption patterns without Western production techniques, urbanization without industrialization, secularization (the decline of religion) without scientification (the rise of science), and capitalist greed without capitalist discipline. The heritage Africa received from the West, then, was a distorted form of capitalism. The problem has not been that Africa has had too much capitalism, but that it wasn't allowed by the colonial experience to have effective, autonomous capitalist growth. Rather, African capitalism has been an appendage of somebody else's capitalism.

We might call this first stage in Africa's economic development the "Euro-African" phase of African capitalism. The question which then arises is whether there is an Americo-African phase of African capitalism. Will the U.S. impact smooth out the distortions caused by Europe? Post-colonial statism in African economies was a continuation of colonial statism in African economies, including huge bureaucracies and expanded marketing boards for African commodities which had been set up by the colonial powers. The American impact, though, has been to reduce the bureaucracies and abolish the marketing boards, and to create more incentives for entrepreneurs and for farmers.

Will it work? I don't know because the second phase of capitalism, the Americo-African phase, has only just begun. Until now it has been true that capitalism's worst enemy in Africa has been the West's own impact there. But is this other part of the West (the U.S.) going to change the situation? We don't know because it is too early.

There is no doubt that privatization is well underway in Africa. The programs of the Reagan legacy, of the World Bank, and of the IMF have all pushed us toward new forms of capitalist experiments. Will they work better than the European versions of capitalism? Again, we must wait and see.

As for the other basic area of American political differentiation, political pluralism (what you call democracy), there is again some tension between the European version and the American version of the West's influence in Africa. What you should bear in mind is that we often take for granted the social underpinnings of democracy. Though we think of democracy politically, it has social roots. So Europeanization at the university level has placed disproportionate emphasis on purely academic matters. American innovations in Africa include more practical forms of higher education. European tendencies focus on primary and secondary schools, and these are still heavily Europeanized. American innovations are beginning at the tertiary and higher levels.

One can even witness the social differences on a popular level. European dress culture is still very formal. The American impact on African dressing patterns has been to make it more casual and to popularize certain styles. For instance, restaurants in Kampala and Nairobi that used to insist I wear a tie have now loosened up, partly because of the impact of American tourists in African cities. In the colonial period it was still possible to go in a restaurant in Kampala and be told, "Sir, you haven't got a tie; I have one to lend you if you want to dine here." I think this is much less the case in Africa now.

There is a difference of impact on the food culture as well. European culture has been elitist, and formal cuisine is in this realm too. If you invited a friend home for dinner during the period of European dominance, the chances are that it would have been formal and European. The American genius for quick food has started the "hamburger revolution" in parts of urban Africa, as witnessed by the Kentucky Fried Chicken franchise in Nairobi. The American impact on alcoholic beverages has been negligible. Nobody has ever heard of bourbon in most of Africa, but everybody has had a Scotch whiskey; French wines are triumphant in former French Africa and are increasingly popular in former British Africa as well. The American culinary genius is not in alcoholic drinks, but in soft drinks—there has been a "Coca-Colanization" of Africa.

While elitist newspapers from Britain or France are read in the car or in Nairobi restaurants, popular news magazines bear the stamp of the *Time-Newsweek* influence across Africa.

What I am suggesting, then, is that elements of Americanization in Africa, though not directly political, are affecting the social roots of politics. The popular impact of American culture may have more relevance for social democratization than we sometimes realize, especially in terms of reduced elitism.

Now let us turn to the actual imitation of the American Constitution. Apart from Liberia, the most notable recent instance of fairly direct imitation was in Nigeria, during Shehu Shagari's reign from 1979 to 1983; this was a deliberate attempt to approximate the American experience. Unfortunately it didn't work, though it did create an open society politically. The years of Shagari were, in fact, probably the most politically open years for Nigeria this century. I heard things said by people in power in Nigeria under Shagari that you wouldn't normally hear elsewhere. Freedom sometimes has even gone mad, not just calling the President a pirate, a thief and a robber, which he was called, but sometimes talking in terms of outright revolution. Economically, this regime was marked by a mad scramble for resources. The treasures of the nation were basically raided right, left, and center, and the country was so impoverished that it has been suffering ever since. So the American system in Shagari's Nigeria did give openness in terms of wide-open dissent, but it also led to sheer economic anarchy. It provided a clear invitation for the military to intervene, and the military did intervene in Nigeria.

Elsewhere in Africa there is often the problem of the dual society, that is, the society where there are two primary groups rather than several. Here the temptation to have a one-party system can help the dual society to insure power-sharing between them. In Zimbabwe, for example, there is not a multiplicity of ethnic groups, but rather a division primarily between the Shona and the Ndebele (Matabele). If most Zimbabweans vote along ethnic lines, and if you have a multiparty system, you will end up with a defacto two-party system. All of the Shona will vote Shona and all Ndebele will vote Ndebele, and since the Shona have a clear and convincing majority, they will always be in power and the Ndebele will always be in opposition. Indeed, this is what happened in the initial years of independence. Now they have decided to try a one-party system to see if they can have more effective power sharing.

The two-party American model in a dual society like Zimbabwe has definite potential to result in violence. Rwanda and Burundi are two similar states within Africa. Outside Africa, there is northern Ireland (Catholic versus Protestant), Cyprus (Greek versus Turkish), and Sri Lanka (Tamil versus Sinhalese). All of them are situations of polarized confrontation without the gift of a dual society. The United States had a dual tendency in the North-South rivalry, though it wasn't a dual society in the same sense; the United States merely had a dual *tendency*, and even that dual tendency in the United States turned out to be explosive. And within the South the one-party loyalty tended to predominate for quite a while after the clash. So there are many countries in Africa where the American model is very hard to adopt, except in regard to presidentialism, which is also part of America's contribution to the whole vocabulary of African politics. Here you control the president with separation of powers, while Africa has often had presidents unrestrained by that. Africa borrowed the secular head of state, but he has been allowed far more power than you allow you own head of state.

My final point concerns the issue of whether there are tendencies towards re-democratization in those African countries which have been struggling to democratize, up until now with a lot of difficulty. And the answer is yes. Sometimes it involves a straight-forward pouring out into the streets to get the bastards out of power; that is the Sudanese model. The Sudanese ever so often use the street riot as a near equivalent to the storming of the Bastille which pulled down the old order. The Sudanese did it way back in 1964, and again in 1985. They actually forced military rulers back to the barracks. Recently they have been rioting, this time against policies. The soldiers do come in every so often when the civilians make a mess, and then the population gets fed up and turns out into the streets.

The opposition in Uganda, unconscious of the American model, but believing that those in power ought to command the loyalty of those they rule, actually formed their own army. They formed a civilian army to fight the army of the rulers, just as Americans had once done in the 18th century. This Ugandan leader was Yoweri Museveni. To fight the army of the state in a situation not involving colonial rule and not involving white minority rule was unique in black Africa, and it was also unique in its success because Museveni did win. I had dinner with him in October 1988 when we had some discussion of what it all meant, and his position was that they overthrew a regime that they regarded as hostile to democratic principles.

America also set an example of succession by voluntary relinquishment of power—George Washington's model if you like. I mentioned Leopold Senghor in Senegal and Julius Nyerere in Tanzania. In fairness I should also mention military rulers like Obasanjo in Nigeria, who also returned to the barracks voluntarily; they have not always been conscious of the Washingtonian precedent, but nevertheless they achieved a transition back to civilian life. And in some cases we have been aware that things were once done by Americans, even if we were not imitating Americans, but rather acting them out ourselves.

The people who made up American political culture, who forged the U.S. Constitution, would seem to have nothing in common with modern Africans: they were white people overwhelmingly male, and many of them unfortunately racist. Some of them, even those as liberal as your revered Jefferson, owned slaves. Yet despite America having a political culture and Constitution structured by a people in conditions radically different from those in Africa, America has nevertheless been recurrently regarded as relevant to the black experience, and the American example has affected aspects of the black experiment in politics. American political genius, then, born out of conditions which included slavery and racism, nevertheless seems to have some relevance for an evolving African civilization.

QUESTION: I had a question about your views on the separation of state and religion in Africa, which is a very interesting topic for us in the United States as well. I agree that it is very important to differentiate between the institutional separation and the cultural separation as you mentioned. Your example of Senghor, though, reminded me of how much access to positions of state was connected to the liberal, Western education of African leaders, especially immediately after the colonial period. In the colonial African experience education went hand in hand with religious ideologies, since most of the early schools were missionary schools. I would argue, then, that Senghor was able to become president of Senegal not so much because Senegalese people made a conscious, deliberate decision to separate religion from politics, but simply because he had the requisite level of Western education that made him eligible, regardless of religion. In fact, in Senegal today, as in much of Africa, where Islamic fundamentalism is re-emerging now, religious behavior is influencing politics again. Nigeria has had cases of that, as has Senegal. The Moslem interest groups have had a lot of impact on the political system, even though they may not necessarily have an official voice in political institutions.

PROFESSOR MAZRUI: Since Senghor was hardly the only Westernized, educated African around, that can't be the explanation. Senegal has just lost Cheikh Anta Diop, who is a bigger intellectual giant to Africans, though not necessarily to Frenchmen, than even Senghor, though Senghor himself is a major intellectual figure. Diop was a physicist, philosopher, man of letters, and Renaissance man who was approximately the same age as Leopold Senghor. He had political ambitions and made a number of attempts even in the early 1980s to attain office, but he didn't make it. Diop was a *Muslim.*

The first response to your question is that it isn't as if the only educated man in Senegal was Leopold Senghor and therefore he was chosen. There were a lot of

Muslims—Diop for instance was a Muslim—who were Muslim-educated Senegalese and still didn't make it.

Secondly, you have a political culture where the fact that Senghor is good in French is more important than the fact that he is not a Muslim. The point would still apply whether you are prepared to concede levels of achievement in the individual candidate—in this case linguistic and literary achievements of Leopold Senghor—as weighty enough to overcome your own preference for a co-religionist. This wouldn't happen in the United States. I'm sure that in the United States there must be a lot of Jews who have been better intellectually than the last ten presidents that this country has had. That has never been enough of a credential for Americans to go for a qualified Jew, though, because the other factors have impeded that.

The final point you raise concerned religion elsewhere in Africa, and you are quite right where religion coincides with ethnic differences, it certainly reinforces preexisting ethnic differences. In Nigeria, for example, almost all Hausa are Muslims, so their being Muslim is an additional factor about their "Hausa-ness." Almost all Ibo are Christian and their being Christian is an additional factor about their "Ibo-ness." The Yoruba are split half Muslim and half Christian. What you have had in Nigeria, then, is a politicization of religion, partly because of the ethnicization of the society. There the situation is almost as bad as in northern Ireland, but not quite as bad as Beirut as yet.

QUESTION: Do you think that was a good idea when Nigerian leaders divided the three southern provinces into smaller provinces or regions along religious lines?

PROFESSOR MAZRUI: It was more promising than having the south face the north as two separate units; in a way Nigeria had the same dualism as Sudan along north-south lines, which was explosive. We should note that the Sudanese were going to divide the north as well, so it wasn't just a case of "divide and rule" but of creating smaller units of localized administration. In terms of its rationality, and especially given Nigeria's experience of having states which were too large and therefore with higher potentiality for confrontation, it seemed to make sense; it's just a pity that in Sudan it was combined with an Islamic crusade at the same time.

In reality, it isn't as if Islamic laws have been especially enforced in Southern Sudan. During my last visit there, you could order drinks in the hotel in the south, which was inconceivable in the north. It is enough to *say* that it applies everywhere, even if you don't actually enforce it; it is enough to create insecurity in the south. So I wasn't comparing just the south with an alternative configuration of religion and ethnicity. I was comparing it with the north-south split.

QUESTION: Do you think the north in Sudan would be wise to let the southerners secede?

PROFESSOR MAZRUI: I don't think that is going to happen, but I have mixed feelings because, like most Africans, I have the worry that if secession succeeds in one place, it can be a sign and a signal to other places. So in the case of Nigeria, one feels that if the Ibo had succeeded, other groups within the Nigerian union would also have wanted to split off.

What I do think is happening now is that the present war in Sudan is not in fact separatist in its intentions, because the southerners now want democratization and justice rather than a separate identity. If the north is wise, it will try a little harder than it seems to be doing, but the government doesn't have much will to be tolerant. The only party within the government which *did* have the will just pulled out of the government three days ago. So unfortunately I don't think secession is likely to happen, and it doesn't have to happen since southerners no longer demand separation; they just demand justice within Sudan.

QUESTION: My question is about the idea of a constitution, that is, what people mean when they talk about "constitutions." In the Western liberal democracies rimming the Atlantic there are various traditions, but I would like to mention especially two. One is the American model in which the Constitution has certain overtones of higher law or natural law, the notion being that certain norms would exist even if you didn't put them into the Constitution document. These ideas are Lockean in origin, if you like. A competing model would be the French model of a constitution, which is more positivistic, showing perhaps the influence of Rousseau's general will. These are not quite the same ways of looking at constitutions, and I mention them simply to ask whether Africans, when they sit down to write constitutions or to interpret them, bring one kind or another of constitutional theory to bear on their situations. If so, does that theory in Francophone Africa owe anything to the French model and do Anglophone African constitution-makers owe anything to the British model?

PROFESSOR MAZRUI: The actual drafters of constitutions have certainly been very conscious of external models, and in Francophone Africa they will be very conscious of what has been attempted in France under the different republics. The Fourth Republic model, although it only lasted until 1958, before much of French Africa became independent, seemed particularly unsuitable for Africa because it was excessively parliamentary and inadequately executive. In fact, 1958 came just in time for Africa because de Gaulle came into power in that year. In 1960 virtually all African countries under French domination became at least nominally independent. And de Gaulle then structured the Fifth Republic with much more executive power than there had been under the Fourth. That change was more relevant for Africa, which was more inclined towards "Bonapartism" than towards any sort of parliamentarism.

In Anglophone Africa the British tradition, although lacking in formal written documents, was omnipresent among legal drafters and constitutional lawyers. They came in at various stages when the constitution-makers were working out the document and infused some of their constitutionalist ideas into the creative process. Whatever the constitution, the *de facto* governments have been much closer to Rousseau's general will model—a kind of legislature that could modify the regime—than they are to the American experience. This is *de facto* not always conscious of the precise French precedent.

QUESTION: A corollary to that question is whether judicial review tends to rise or fall with those models.

PROFESSOR MAZRUI: Judicial review, as you can imagine, has had a tough time in Africa partly because of "neo-Bonapartism" and the triumph of the will of the people as against a collection of judges at any particular time. There are exceptions, though. Nigeria has built up more of a body of constitutional law than average partly because of its size, partly because of its federalism, and partly because it has such huge numbers of lawyers by African standards! But in other countries, although there is an element of judicial review, the traditions of the imperial power were themselves ones which reduce the role of the courts. Even in Britain, for example, the courts are much more subordinate to the political process than they are in the United States. In general, then, there is not yet an established and stable judicial order.

QUESTION: Is there anything to be learned from the confederate experience in Cameroon, where a Francophone entity and an Anglophone entity have joined in a federation? I was there in the 1960s, but I have lost track of what has happened since. It's still together, isn't it? There must have been a lot of divisive possibilities there.

PROFESSOR MAZRUI: Until recently it was a relative success story, and not just in terms of the union between the parts which were previously ruled by France and Britain, respectively. In spite of this translingual integration, it also had an above average record in economic performance. Until recently, it was well above average record in political performance and in terms of domestic stability.

The 1980s have been less happy for it, and there has been some decline in political stability and more difficulties in economic performance than there were before. So they have no room for complacency. It still remains an interesting laboratory of translingual integration, albeit an unequal translingual integration.

QUESTION: Is the university still bilingual in Yaounde?

PROFESSOR MAZRUI: It is semibilingual, in the sense that French still has a bigger role in it than English. So the possibility of a "Cameroonian Quebec" in the reverse—dominant French and minority English—is definitely there.

QUESTION: You didn't mention Marxism in your review, and you said that Western capitalism in some way was its own worst enemy. I wonder if you would comment on the challenge of Marxism to American constitutional and economic ideas.

PROFESSOR MAZRUI: If you mean specifically Marxism and not socialism at large, there is a different answer to this question. Marxism is very popular among intellectuals in much of Africa; it is an important alternative paradigm that enables Africans to explore possibilities of intellectual autonomy and rebellion against the Western heritage and to express anti-imperialism. There are a number of specifically Marxist governments. Curiously enough, virtually all countries previously ruled by Britain have avoided Marxism as a basis of government. Practically all countries previously ruled by Portugal adopted Marxism at least for part of their independence period. Countries previously ruled by France are mixed. To summarize, then, you have Portuguese-speaking Africa with much greater proclivity towards Marxism than average, Anglophone Africa with a much more restricted tendency towards Marxism than average, and Francophone Africa with a mixed record. It is interesting to try and determine how much emphasis we should put on the nature of the different impacts of the imperial order, and how much we should put on the other conditions in those societies themselves.

That isn't why I distinguish Marxism from socialism, though. Socialism is a wider term, of which Marxism is only one school. And in a place like Tanzania, which hasn't been Marxist in its experiment at all, there is a commitment to a kind of socialism. Julius Nyerere is very conscious of Marx; he has read a lot of Marxism, but he is consciously non-Marxist. Africans often emphasize that you can be non-Marxist without being anti-Marxist, just as you can be non-Buddhist without being anti-Buddhist. You just look at it as an alternative school of thought.

Socialism itself is more widely popular than Marxism, even in English-speaking Africa. Marxism has a more specialized constituency.

QUESTION: My question is centered on the system of government in Africa as a whole. It is safe to say that our system of government [in Nigeria] has been primarily borrowed from Europe, and from America, but particularly from Europe. For example, we tried to adopt a parliamentary system in 1960 and it failed. Then we tried the American model, and that failed too. I wonder if African intellectuals like you can give us a kind of model taken from the history of an individual country in Africa that might work.

In Nigeria we are trying to establish another constitutional order, and for all I know we are going to repeat the same kinds of efforts and make the same mistakes. Do you think that all of the European models of civil government that we have been practicing are not right for us? What do you think is actually wrong in this system; are we lacking the proper constitutional model, or are we simply failing to properly implement the government?

PROFESSOR MAZRUI: That's a tough one. My own belief is that there is a "curse of the ancestors." I sometimes mean this literally, but I also sometimes mean it metaphorically. The actual deal we made in Africa with the 20th century did not take into account enough of the preceding heritage that we had accumulated. Initially there was almost cultural self-contempt so that there were inadequate allowances for the usages of the indigenous population and for what had been sanctified by time. To punish us it is almost as if the ancestors are saying, "Look here, your constitutions will collapse; your roads will decay; your railway systems will rust; your telephones will go silent; your money will become worthless; your warriors periodically will overthrow your scribes; and you will wander in the wilderness looking for an alternative refuge." Why, we ask? Because we were insensitive to what went before.

In a way, we don't have as yet constitutional engineers who are at the same time immersed in the sociology and anthropology of Africa. We certainly don't have politicians as yet who are sufficiently respectful of our heritage. And until we do, we will continue to have constitutions that are a bit too artificial to work, too unrelated, and therefore too vulnerable to the "curse of the ancestors."

What I recommend to our constitution-makers and to our governments, then, is a transformation so that we regard feasibility studies, not just as matters of economic feasibility, but also of cultural feasibility. They must go and check it out, see whether a given system makes sense given the configuration of people in a certain society. Unfortunately, our governments don't listen to us so, we have a struggle ahead of us.

QUESTION: My question is about the economic crisis which is going on in sub-Saharan Africa. Despite the crisis, governments are paying debts to some corporations or governments which had previously made loans to them. Is it possible for these governments to default rather than commit political suicide? Much of the money that could have been used for social projects in time of crisis has been used instead to pay external agencies or corporations. Is it more politically viable for these governments to default on those loans and take care of the social and economic needs on a temporary basis, negotiating repayment with the international corporations, or continue to pay these loans while these cumulative effects mount up to the point that their stability is threatened.

PROFESSOR MAZRUI: It is an issue which has concerned policy-makers, but no African leader except Julius Nyerere of Tanzania has taken a public position on how you can use indebtedness as power. In a way your question touches on that. If I owe my little bank in Ann Arbor, Michigan $10,000, I'm in trouble, because $10,000 is a lot of money to me. On the other hand, if I owe my little bank in Ann Arbor $50 million, then the bank is in trouble! There is a scale of indebtedness that makes the creditor as vulnerable as the debtor. The question is not necessarily whether we actually do default, but whether we find ways of using the power of indebtedness more effectively to get better terms. We shall really need the support of Latin American countries, because they have huge debts. Brazil alone owes more than the whole of black Africa added together. If we can get the Latin American countries to join forces, we can have a union of the indebted. The cry will be, "indebted of the world unite."

COMMENT: The United States is the biggest debtor of all, though; don't forget that!

PROFESSOR MAZRUI: Yes, I know. You are both the biggest debtor and the biggest creditor, so we have to watch the dualism of the American personality. In general, though, the question does raise important issues for the indebted countries, which is how to get better terms, what forms of pressure to put on the creditors, and whether their very vulnerability of being in debt can be transformed into an instrument of leverage or influence. Julius Nyerere has raised the possibility. Individual Latin American leaders have also used it from time to time. Combining the forces of Africa and the forces of Latin American could help do the trick, not be defaulting necessarily, but by threatening to default.

NARRATOR: Professor Miller, you may ask the last question if you wish; we've had only one sentence about Portuguese Africa.

QUESTION: I'm afraid the question that I would ask would open up a whole new range of discussion, though you've commented eloquently on a number of aspects of American influence in sub-Saharan Africa. The country that makes most explicit and sometimes propagandistic use of parallels with the United States, of course, is the Republic of South Africa. I wondered if you had any final comment to make on the ideas that you have been offering this morning with regard to South Africa.

PROFESSOR MAZRUI: As you know, the whites in South Africa tend to present themselves as a kind of bastion of democracy and therefore part of the heritage that is shared with the United States. It is a democracy that is racially selective; it is internally racist. Moreover, it doesn't even have the advantage that the United States had in the first phase that I mentioned when the United States was domestically racist and externally anti-colonialist. South Africa is internally racist and externally pro-colonialist, and in fact itself a mini-imperial power in the subregion. Unfortunately, I don't see the possibility of a change without considerable violence. There is no precedent in Africa of a well-established minority white population giving up power without a kind of war. We went through it in Kenya, in fact, when the population was only 1 percent white. Algeria had something like 10 percent; Zimbabwe had 15 percent, etc. South Africa has an even bigger proportion of whites. In short, I don't see a solution without the agony of war. I only hope it is not as costly in human lives as was the Algerian war, which cost a million lives. Algeria is the nearest equivalent in terms of disproportion of power, that is, the disproportion between French power in Algeria and the FLN fighting for independence. This is the nearest equivalent to blacks in South Africa fighting against white military supremacy. But let's hope that the cost in South Africa won't be on that Algerian scale; there will be a cost, though, I suspect in the 1990s. And if we are lucky, it may be of short duration and will be all over by the end of the century.

NARRATOR: On that note we will stop, but we want to thank Professor Mazrui very much for coming here. An idiot could have identified him as a most promising intellectual even when he was a young student, but it is always nice to know that one wasn't too much of an idiot. It is a great pleasure and privilege to have you with us.

Constitutionalism in Africa*

IBRAHIM A. GAMBARI

NARRATOR: One thing I missed most in leaving an international foundation was the important and fruitful contact with the emerging leadership of Third World Countries that I used to have at the Rockefeller Foundation. After a rather vigorous debate, I remember one young leader saying, "Don't you know that we are your friends? We were trained in your universities; we share your values. Our relations with others are obviously important, but for the next hundred years the relationship with the West is even more important." I think that the friendships, knowledge, and exchange of ideas that grow out of these ties which some maintain with African leaders, could prove to be as crucial to the future of international civilization as anything else. I say that by way of introduction because, in our series on constitutionalism, the development of constitutionalism in Africa certainly matches in importance the development of constitutional government in any other part of the world.

In that development scholars such as Dr. Ibrahim Gambari of Ahmadu Bello University in Zaria, will play a very central role. His development in a sense is representative of the pattern I've just mentioned. He was born in Ilorin in the mid-central region of Nigeria, received his secondary education at King's College, Lagos, and then by-passed Ibadan and other Nigerian universities to study at the London School of Economics. He went on to Columbia University in the era of James Sterling Young, and

Presented in a forum at the Miller Center on May 16, 1988.

indeed studied in the same Government Department in which Jim Young was a professor. Finally, he received the doctorate degree for a dissertation on the relationship between domestic and international politics as determinants in Nigerian foreign policy.

From there he went on to teach, first at the State University of New York in Albany where Gray Cowan, a former professor at Columbia, was dean of the Graduate School of Public Affairs. He returned to Nigeria and taught for a time in Ahmadu Bello and then became the director general of the Institute of International Affairs in Lagos. After that he served for eighteen months as foreign minister in the federal government. Then he returned to academia, his first love and his first interest—on one occasion he made the comment that he spent most of his life studying and teaching—and took up teaching and research responsibilities in the U.S. once more. He has taught most recently at Johns Hopkins University's School for Advanced International Studies in Washington where he collaborated with Professor I. William Zartman. He has also been at the Woodrow Wilson Center in Washington. He is working on two books: one on theory and practice in foreign policy-making, which will be published by Humanities Press, N.J., in February 1989, and another in the general area of constitutionalism in Africa.

PROFESSOR GAMBARI: Thank you very much for that wonderful introduction. I could add a story to that introduction. When my father learned that I had been admitted to Columbia University in 1968, he said, "Well, you surely know how to pick your universities," because the London School of Economics was then in crisis. I managed to get a degree before it was completely closed down and then I went to Columbia in 1968, and of course you know that it was undergoing a crisis of its own. Despite the turmoil, it was a good experience because at the end of it all, I could identify a set of values that is shared closely by my country and the United States and Britain.

Nigeria was a former British colony, which gained its independence in 1960. But we are also a country in a hurry. We want to experiment with other peoples' systems, other peoples' values, and in doing so, we of course encounter a lot of problems, but also a lot of healthy challenges. Nigeria is the most populous country in Africa; the population is estimated now at about 110 million, which means that one out of every five Africans is a Nigerian. Therefore what happens in Nigeria has a tremendous impact on Africa, not just because of the demographic reality, but also because Nigerians tend to see themselves as leaders in the continent's affairs. Moreover, I think many countries in Africa sometimes grudgingly accept that perception of Nigeria. It is Nigeria's future and role as a bellwether of Africa that I would like to discuss.

This is an interesting time for such a discussion because our nation may be near another milestone in constitutionalism and constitutional process as the country is presently engaged in implementing a political program aimed at the restoration of constitutional rule by the year 1992. This is in a real sense the third attempt to establish the basis for constitutional rule in Nigeria. The first attempt took place under the umbrella and supervision of the colonial authorities in the 1940s and 1950s, the decades preceding the independence of Nigeria. The British were preparing us for constitutional rule by trying to identify the new leadership and institutionalize the process of the government that was going to take over from the British.

The second and third attempts at constitutional rule were undertaken by military regimes, which respectively overthrew the First and Second Republics in Nigeria. I will explain this in more detail later. First, though, I would make the point that the two architects of constitutional rule in Nigeria, that is the British colonial authorities and then the military rulers, were themselves non-democratic forces. It is very significant that those who were interested in organizing constitutional rule and constitutionalism were themselves non-democratic authorities.

The fact that the colonial authorities and the military rulers in Nigeria were more or less compelled to establish the process leading to their replacement by elected representatives illustrates the lack of legitimacy of colonial rule and the lack of legitimacy of military rule in Nigeria. No one with power gives it up voluntarily. So the argument I'm making is that the colonial rulers and the military rulers in Nigeria are comparable in that both were perceived as illegitimate as rulers and both had to prepare the way for a constitutional, democratic rule.

This leads to a second question, that of whether autocratic rulers can organize a successful transition to a durable democratic government. This is a highly philosophical question and I have some tentative ideas on this. It may well be that the imperfections of the constitutional system in Nigeria are in part a reflection of the fact that those who prepared the country for democratic processes were themselves nondemocratic institutions—that is, colonial rulers and then military leaders.

Whether we accept that theory or not, the fact is that the democratic experiments which followed colonial rule and the return of the military rulers to the barracks both failed miserably. The responsibility for the failures, however, could not be pinned upon the architects of the constitutions alone, but also on the structure of the constitutional processes themselves, the elected operators of the system, and the domestic, social, economic, cultural and even external environment within which the democratic experiments took place. Those experiments in democratic rule prepared first by the colonial administration and then by the military rulers in Nigeria failed, but the blame should not be pinned entirely on the colonial powers themselves or on the military rulers. Perhaps the responsibility lies within the system which they left behind, with the operators themselves, and, of course, with the environment in which all these constitutional developments took place.

Given this background, I would like to share some further thoughts on the prospects and difficulties of the process of constitutionalism in Nigeria. I'd also like to look at the influence of Western thought on the constitutional processes and development in Nigeria and Africa, and perhaps ask as well in what way has Nigerian constitutional experimentation influenced Western thought? What have we done that is perhaps a step forward from what we inherited from western constitutional thought?

Let me begin by suggesting that the pluralism of Nigerian society and the irrepressible democratic spirit of our people requires an arrangement for constitutional rule. Let me give you a very short illustration. Idi Amin, the notoriously autocratic ruler of Uganda, came to visit Nigeria during the time that Nigeria was ruled by the military. He looked at the newspapers in Nigeria, and saw that one of them, which was owned by the government, featured a very severe critique of Idi Amin's rule. Amin was outraged and ran to the host head-of-state, who was also a military ruler, and complained, "How can this happen? I am a guest in your country and your government paper is criticizing me during my visit!" The Nigerian head-of-state replied, "Well, I'm sorry about that," and he then asked his aide to bring him a copy of the previous day's paper. In that same government paper there was an article condemning our own head of state. Idi Amin then said, "And you call this a military regime?"

There are now about twenty-six daily newspapers in Nigeria, most of them owned by government, and yet they are often extremely critical of the government. This is what I call an illustration of the democratic spirit that cannot be repressed, and therefore autocratic regimes in Nigeria can never be regarded as legitimate, nor can they really be workable for any length of time. It is an interesting paradox that the only way a non-elected military regime in Nigeria can survive is for it to say, "We are on our way out." In effect, the rulers have to say, "We are not here to stay. The regime is temporary, and as soon as it fulfills the mission that brought it into power as a corrective kind of regime, the military rulers are going to go." The only way such unelected regimes can stay is to be perceived as temporary rule. There is an absolute demand on the part of the Nigerian people for an elected and constitutional regime.

The second major point that I would like to make here is that despite the many military coups, there has been underlying stability in Nigeria. There have been five successful military coups in Nigeria that have overthrown either elected civilian regimes or military regimes. Those latter type we might call palace coups. Moreover, there have been several unsuccessful coup attempts, but in spite of these coups, there has been underlying political stability in the country. It may seem to be a contradiction. If there is a coup tomorrow, casual observers will say, "Oh, there goes another coup in Nigeria; this is a very unstable country." In fact there is underlying political stability, irrespective of these coups. This is partly because of the democratic spirit that prevents extremes of autocracy, even under a military regime. It is also because there is a loose coalition of interests and forces in Nigeria: the bureaucracy, which is very strong; business, which reflects free enterprise; the military leaders; the political elite and the traditional rulers in the country. This relatively loose coalition actually keeps things going, irrespective of these many coups.

This loose coalition of elites that keeps the country going is very important and necessary because it is the only way to sustain the unity and territorial integrity of Nigeria. But this underlying political stability presents both challenges and opportunities for constitutionalism and durable democratic rule in Nigeria. After all, compromise and consensus are elements of constitutional rule, and that underlying stability within the nation is a reflection of the consensus and compromise of the various groups and regions within Nigeria. Therefore, it presents the hope for the establishment of a durable constitutional regime. However, there are tiny fringes that are against consensus, against compromise, and against the coalition of domestic political forces. Unfortunately, they are gaining strength. The attraction of extremism is growing, both as an instrument and as a body of belief and it poses real dangers to political stability and the rule of law in Nigeria. I am going to discuss what I mean by the rising tide of extremism which has religious as well as political elements. Let me examine the three elements in the equation of constitutional reform in Nigeria before coming to some of my conclusions.

First, let me pose a problem. The elected government that replaced the departing British colonial authorities, lasted from October 1960 to January 1966; that's very important. That was our First Republic. On the face of it, the transition from the British colonial rule to what seemed to be a moderate government of independent Nigeria, appeared to be relatively peaceful and orderly. As a matter of fact, the world had an extremely favorable image of Nigeria. The young President Kennedy, for example, looked at Nigeria in 1960 and thought that here was a potentially strong and stable black African nation. At that time our population amounted to about 30 or 40 million people and Kennedy thought that, if it were united, peaceful and democratic, Nigeria would be an ally of the West. He saw Nigeria as a country to be cultivated. If the United States could also cultivate India, the largest democracy in Asia and the world, then America would be in good company. Nigeria, it was hoped, would be the model of democracy in Africa. That perception of a democratic Nigeria, a process with which we were really only experimenting after having just emerged from colonial rule, was stronger outside than inside Nigeria.

The high hopes and expectations for democratic and durable constitutional rule in Nigeria were soon dashed, and there were four main reasons for the unsatisfactory political situation which led to the demise of that Republic and its overthrow by the military. The first reason was that the central government itself was not really accepted by the various ethnic and ideological groups in Nigeria because the central government was a tentative and very uneasy coalition of two political parties, both of which were largely ethnically based. They were not able to transcend parochial concerns of their constituents, let alone define national policies and interests. Therefore, they began to lose legitimacy in the eyes of the other political parties that were not part of the government. Since political parties of the First Republic represented little more than ethnic interests, so those in power felt a sense of pride and opportunity. Those that were out of power, felt neglected and began to despise the central government.

Second, the regions were too powerful in relation to the central government. Most of the political party leaders stayed in their regions rather than going to the center because that is where their privileges were. That's where their power was. And because they did not leave the regions for the center, the center was much weaker than the outlying territories. In terms of building political leadership and national unity, this was a very big handicap indeed. Also, regions coincided not only with the domain of major ethnic groups in Nigeria, like the Ibos in the East, the Yorubas in the West and the Hausa in the North, but each of these ethnic groups has a population greater than the majority of African countries. Each of them has more than ten million people, which is a huge number if we consider that twenty five of about fifty African countries have a population of five million or less.

The third major reason why the First Republic failed was the failure of the government to provide decisive leadership even at the most crucial times. Of course, this was due in part to the problem of forming stable coalitions, because we had a parliamentary system. You have to govern; you have to have a parliamentary majority. None of the major parties of that time had enough seats in parliament to rule by majority, so they had to rule by coalition. You don't get decisive leadership running a coalition government. Problems also arose because of the personality and political style of the first prime minister whom we had in Nigeria, Sir Abubakar Tafawa Balewa, who was a man of compromise and conciliation. His problems mounted when the mood of the country began to change from compromise to confrontation and conflict. That regime ended in violence, as a number of you here, I am sure, know. A full-scale civil war ensued soon after the collapse of the First Republic.

Finally, the "Westminster" parliamentary model of government was a factor in the downfall of the first experimental democracy. You are familiar with that model in which the winner takes everything and the loser goes into the opposition. In a country of plural ethnic and religious groups, that model was incapable of aggregating their various interests. In our tradition, official loyal opposition simply cannot occur. Loyal opposition may work in her Majesty's British parliament but it did not in Nigeria where consensus and unity are long-standing African values. In our system, you are either in or out; there is no question of loyalty of the opposition. Therefore, there was no commitment on the part of the opposition to the rules of the game; nor was there a commitment on the part of the government parties to act fairly toward the opposition.

As a result of all these factors, then, the first experiments with constitutional process collapsed. The first elected regime fell victim to the military, which ruled for thirteen years, from 1966 to 1979. Fortunately, as I said earlier, no matter how long the military stays in power, Nigerians will not accept it as a permanent or legitimate form of rule. The military, then, had to prepare for a return to civilian rule and they had a political program starting in 1976 that culminated in 1979 when Nigeria was returned to civilian rule once more, and we had the inauguration of our Second Republic.

The Second Republic or the second experiment in the democratic rule lasted from 1979 to 1983. By the time the civilian authorities were elected and came into power, the structure of the country appeared to be much better than in the decade of independence, in the 1960s. I can give you some illustrations of how the polity, the state structure, was much stronger in 1979 than it was in 1960. On the face of it, there were greater opportunities for the establishment of democracy in Nigeria in 1979 than in 1960. By this time secession by any part of Nigeria was no longer considered to be a viable option; we had gone through a bitter civil war. People had decided that if there was a problem between the ethnic groups or the regions, they would just have to sit down and talk it out; secession was not the answer. Before then, any time there was a disagreement between groups, the feeling was, "OK, we'll go it alone," but the tragedy of the civil war convinced everybody that this approach was wrong and no longer tenable.

Secondly, instead of three, or a little later, four powerful regions confronting a weak center, by 1979 the country was subdivided first into twelve states and later into nineteen states. This reorganization, of course, served to strengthen the center because the center was the focus of unity. So nobody in the region was powerful enough to challenge the center. This also created some new problems later. None of the new states were financially strong enough to say, "To hell with the center." They are now very dependent on the central government for revenue, even to pay salaries of their workers. This can be considered a problem because we operate under a federal system. When you reduce the states to total dependence on the central government for revenues, then your federal structure is out of balance. But in terms of national political stability, the reform has been beneficial.

The third aspect that helped us in terms of structural strength for the basis of democracy in 1976 as opposed to 1960 was the state of the economy. By 1979 the incoming, elected administration inherited a surplus in foreign reserves of $3 billion in U.S. currency. At that time, too, the country was producing and exporting petroleum very profitably. We were producing two million barrels of oil a day and selling it for $40 a barrel, thus making $80 million a day. By African standards, or by any standard, that was a helpful development. (We miss that income now because the United States is not paying as much for our oil now as it used to. I think the price of oil now is about $18 per barrel.) Anyway, $80 million a day was a lot of money for the politicians to spend. What they did with it was not very wise and it contributed to their downfall. When the money was there to spend, the structure of state was holding up better.

Finally the new constitution of 1979-83, modeled after the presidential system of the United States, was a potential plus. This is very important because the parliamentary system was not really suitable for the pluralistic society and large territory of a country like Nigeria. We needed a kind of presidential system. What are the advantages? I don't need to go into detail here. You have many power centers. The president can come from one party; the Congress can be controlled by another, so everybody shares power. The committee system in Congress was found to be very useful. Also you can have one party controlling the central government and other parties controlling the state legislatures and the state executives. In this way, you give everybody a sense of belonging, and we found that very useful.

As a matter of fact, we then went a step beyond that of the United States Constitution. We required the election of our president under a system that is far more stringent than that of electing the United States president. The president must not only get the plurality of the popular vote, but he must also get not less than 25 percent of the votes in at least two-thirds of the states of the federation. You can see what that means. That means nobody can be elected if he has appeal in only one section of the country. You have to have a broad base of support; you have to be a real symbol of national unity and national integration, which is not easy. The presidential candidates in 1979, campaigned like they had never done before. In contrast to the parliamentary system, where to become prime minister all you have to do is to get elected in your small parliamentary district and be part of a majority party in parliament, the president has to be elected by a broad national constituency. We hoped these changes would be the pillars of a more durable constitutional process in Nigeria. If Nigeria could succeed with a constitutional system that is durable, then that would be a good example for the rest of the African continent.

Unfortunately the high hopes for constitutionalism, engendered by all the structural engineering we had done between the demise of the First Republic and the rise of the Second Republic, were dashed by the practitioners of the Second Republic. By the end of their first term in 1983, the country's political class, as it were, had developed very serious credibility problems which would prove fatal for their regime. Remember that it was the military that had organized the civilian elections of 1979. Now it was the turn of the civilians to conduct another set of elections after four years in power, and they proved incapable of conducting them fairly. Perhaps that leads us to the conclusion that to really consolidate our constitutional process, we would need some kind of a referee to conduct the elections. What form could it take? I don't know. The military? Because civilian government proved incapable, unwilling, or both to conduct the elections properly, the legitimacy of the various parties was already ruined when they took their seats as "victors."

Secondly, the ruling elite during its term was unable or unwilling to manage the economy properly and steer it in any positive or clearly discernable direction. It was a real mess. Here was a country that had $3 billion in reserves in 1978, and was making $80 million a day. That revenue went up between 1979 and 1981. While the price of oil declined somewhat from 1981 to 1983, it never went below $25 per barrel. You won't believe that by the end of the Second Republic, when the civilians were overthrown, the politicians had saddled Nigeria with $22 billion in debts and made Nigeria one of the major debtor nations in Africa. All this happened in only four years.

The third serious problem that the civilian rulers faced was the practice of official corruption and total lack of accountability. This was not a new problem, but the heights to which official corruption and lack of responsibility rose were unprecedented in the history of the country, perhaps because we had never made so much money in so little time. Finally, the civilian regime was terminated in December of 1983 and the military came back to power once again, first under General Buhari in January of 1984 to August of 1985—that was the regime in which I served as foreign minister—and later General Babangida. Even the military regime realized that they needed civilian people to help them run the country and to buy them legitimacy. So they asked someone like myself, who was not a soldier, to be in the Cabinet. There were several of us civilians whom they chose, because they felt we had some credibility in our respective constituencies—academia in my case, and business and technical sectors in some others.

The military regime that I served was overthrown by another military regime which is still in power, but that regime has quickly learned a lesson that others have internalized before; that is, they too, must prepare the country for a return to civilian rule one more time, to lay the foundation for the Third Republic, which is supposed to be established in 1990. The process has already started and it is supposed to culminate in total return to civilian rule by 1992. So we are now looking forward to the establishment of the Third Republic.

You may well ask, will this republic go the same way as the First and Second Republics? The present military rulers say "no," and if you ask "why," they reply that they are taking measures to see to it that the Third Republic does not fail the way the previous ones have. You may also ask what are the things they can do to put the Third Republic is built on a much more solid foundation? First, they agreed to go back and examine the federal system of national government, state government, and local government, and determine where the real source of authority is in Nigeria. So last December they had elections at the local government level, on a non-party basis. It was hoped that people would contest with each other on their own merits, not as members of political parties. This would help the people to know who at the local level is good, not corrupt, and serves the public interest. The rest of the federal system is built on that. We will start with the introduction of party politics from the local level to elections for the state legislatures, followed by elections to the state governor's houses, the national legislature, and finally the presidency. Again we've decided to retain the United States type of constitution.

Secondly, the military government set up a Political Bureau. The name which sounds like the "politburo" of the Soviet Union or some other communist country, is hardly congruent with a search for a democratic regime. However, the job of the political bureau was to analyze what was wrong with our past politics and to seek solutions: How do we go forward from there? The Bureau proceeded to interview people all over the country, in public hearings held in the towns. Based upon the collected data, the bureau wrote a report and submitted it to the government. The government looked at it, and rejected some things which were too idealistic perhaps because the bureau was dominated by political or social scientists from Nigerian universities. In fact, the Bureau recommended, among other things, that Nigeria should go socialist. The government wisely said "no" to that because it did not want to impose any ideology on the people. It thought that ideology should evolve as it will.

The government accepted the Bureau's report and set up a constitutional review committee to prepare a document to be considered by a Constituent Assembly. The Assembly, representing a variety of interests in Nigeria is to come out with a revised constitution, based on the American model. The Assembly is to recommend measures to perfect the document and to prevent future abuses. Once again an attempt is being made to involve the people in the process instead of handing down the constitution from above.

There is a third problem, which is to identify those who have held top political positions in the past or have been found guilty of misuse of public funds or irresponsibility with the public trust. The government has prohibited them from contesting for public office the next time around. These are problems touching on fundamental human rights. The government is saying, though, that this is the price we have to pay for orderly government. It wants to give a chance to a new generation of politicians, who are not tainted, to run the new system. That doesn't mean that former public officials are banned for life to stay out of politics; it just means that they cannot take part in the next set of elections. A new lease on life is to be given to the political process. All these maneuvers are attempts to improve on previous efforts and to establish a more durable foundation for the Third Republic by 1992.

There are a number of other critical issues in the constitutional process which I would like to mention. They are very sensitive issues that could frustrate a smooth transition to constitutional rule in Nigeria, or weaken constitutional rule once it is established. Let me point out a few.

First, there is the role of local and traditional authorities. We have not decided what we want to do with the traditional rulers in Nigeria. This is a problem that is widespread in Africa. Traditional rulers are those who are not elected, but who enjoy tremendous influence in their various localities, tribes, or, if you prefer, districts. Under a strict democratic constitution, they should have no role at all. The key problem is to have peace between the modern and the historical figures of our country. To shut them out is to reduce chances for domestic peace, and yet how are they to be included? If there were only one king in Nigeria, one traditional ruler, then we could make him or her the king or queen of Nigeria much like the British monarch, and then he or she could be head of state with all the prestige but no power. On the contrary, we have several traditional rulers. How to include them in the democratic process has not been very seriously addressed.

Secondly, the long years of military rule in Nigeria have caused problems. You will recall that I mentioned that the military first came to power in January of 1966 and stayed for about thirteen years, until October of 1979. Then they came back again in January of 1984, and they are still around and will probably be around until 1992. As a result, the process of constitutionalism in Nigeria is suspended and with it the process of trial and error. The cumulative learning experience of party politics and constitutional rule has been less than it would have been because of prolonged military rule. The rules of the political game have not been given much chance to emerge and be internalized. Even the banning of some people from holding political office next time around poses some problems because it excludes them from the political process. Many of them may be corrupt but some of them are not corrupt. I think democracy by itself does not eliminate the problem of corruption. In fact, democracy can corrupt, because when you get funding for political parties to campaign, post-election favors are often exchanged for the contributions. There is, after all, a certain level of corruption in this country; look at Queens, or Washington, D.C., or the financing of the presidential campaigns. It is really a question of what degree of corruption will be tolerated in any given society. People always skirt the boundaries of the law. But if you limit political participation, political parties are going to lose followers and without political parties you cannot have a constitutional, democratic system. You cannot have a party-less democracy.

Thirdly, the population issue is important for Nigeria. We have not had a very successful census since independence, but not for want of trying. In other words, we really don't know exactly how many people Nigeria has. It is not because we can't count, but because often we don't want to know how many people live in one region as opposed to another. We don't really want to know how many Muslims there are as opposed to how many Christians because these are extremely divisive issues. And yet, without an accurate population count, we have such problems as compiling accurate voter registrations, constituency delineation, and so on. This regime has to take the bull by the horns—I believe it wants to do that—and conduct a population census, before the restoration of constitutional rule in 1992. We must know precisely what the population balance is for the election as well as for other things, such as economic planning.

And last, but far from being the least critical issue, is the threat to the continued existence of Nigeria as a secular state. It is my belief, that you cannot have constitutional rule or rule of law without a secular state. The moment you try to impose a religious order on the political life of a country, you have problems. I'm afraid that the Islamic fundamentalists in Nigeria are growing in number. There are probably more Muslims in Nigeria than there are Christians and they are located mostly in the northern regions. The Islamic fundamentalists in the North are not saying that they reject secular rule, but that Islam does not allow for separation of church and state. They say that they would like to establish an Islamic state in Nigeria. If they insist on that and they become strong and powerful enough to insist on it, then Nigeria, as we know it, will simply disintegrate, because there are people who would not go along with it. There are many Christians and there are others, who do not belong to either faith, in Nigeria. This is extremely critical. We've had religious clashes in 1980-81, 1984, 1985 and 1986 where lives were lost. That kind of religious intolerance is not good for the give and take, consensus building and compromise that are the hallmark of a democratic constitutional system. So far, the state has refused to give in to the demands of the Islamic fundamentalists, but the Islamic fundamentalists have also refused to give up their demands. We have a kind of stalemate at the moment. It seems to me, even though I'm a Muslim, that if we don't retain the secular state in Nigeria, then we can say goodbye to the prospect of constitutionalism.

Why has religious fundamentalism increased? There is a linkage, I think, between radical Islamic fundamentalists and the growing number of unemployed Nigerians. They are alienated by economic stagnation. This is where I think the West could help. The IMF has come up with a dramatic plan that we have to implement to reform our economy: devalue the currency, open the gate to imports, reduce subsidies to social services, etc. But this creates hardships for people. If the IMF, the World Bank and the Western countries with whom we have close economic ties, don't re-examine their policies, the effect will be a growing army of hungry people. They will be very angry people and very anti-Western people who will team up with Islamic fundamentalists. Don't forget about the link with Iran, which is violently anti-West. With an Islamic state in Nigeria we would really have problems. As of now, we are a secular, potentially democratic state with hopes of maintaining a good relationship with the United States because of our shared values.

Let me conclude with the comment that the forces promoting democracy and free enterprise remain very strong in Nigeria. As long as they remain strong and we encourage them, we will ultimately guarantee the establishment of constitutional government in the country. Having made this optimistic remark, one still has to ask, "When will we have this durable constitutional government in Nigeria? How is this going to be established and by whom?" This remains the challenge facing Nigeria. In dealing with it, we will continue to borrow from the constitutional experience of the United States and other Western countries. However, until we arrive at the proper balance between those ideas and practices which we borrow from outside and those we derive from our own realities and cultural experiences to take control of the process of constitutionalism in Nigeria, the dream of constitutionalism will continue to be just that, a dream. But the good thing is that it need not be a dream. The dream will come nearer to fruition when an elected civilian regime successfully conducts a free and fair election next time around.

I want to close by recalling a conversation I once had with the Secretary-General of the United Nations, Javier Perez de Cuellar. He was visiting the government of Nigeria in January 1984. I had been in office just one week as foreign minister and here I was receiving the Secretary-General of the United Nations. You can imagine how intimidating that was. But he was a very nice and very relaxed man. He told us that he comes from Peru and that people used to say that Peru is a potentially powerful, rich and democratic country, but that they had been saying that for the last two hundred years. Then he expressed his hope that the same thing would not be true of Nigeria. I hope so too, and I believe that we can succeed in our constitutional experiment the third time around. This would be a good example for Africa, but it would also be good for the future relations among Nigeria, Africa, the United States and Western Europe.

COMMENT: That was a fascinating series of comments on Nigeria's recent political history, but also a very broad and profound analysis of political issues in modern Africa. In the latter connection I was interested in your recognition of the significance of the so-called "traditional" authorities, who I would agree are very important. Perhaps, though, you contradicted yourself when you referred to religious politics near the end. I see many of those traditional groups as having a religious basis for their identity, so communal politics and religious politics are not separable. You said that those religious groups should not acquire an undue influence in a democratic, secular state which is fundamentally individual as opposed to communal in nature. I wonder if there is anything further to be said about your initial acknowledgement of the importance of the traditional group, and your concluding emphasis on excluding religion from a role of government.

PROFESSOR GAMBARI: You are absolutely right. There are two comments I'd like to make. First, the traditional rulers in Nigeria are of a wide variety, though obviously we have lumped them together. In the northern part of Nigeria where the majority of the Muslims live, the traditional rulers are in fact the products of an earlier theocracy and so their religious education was extremely profound. That was not necessarily the case with many of the other traditional rulers in the southern part of Nigeria where the source of authority is more culturally and less religiously based. Even in the north where the authority of the traditional rulers has historically been religious and is expected to perform important political functions, it has been more or less democraticized over the years. Many reforms have really addressed themselves to prevent religious authorities from performing overtly political functions. In other words, the reforms try to return them to the role of being the fathers of their communities and allies of national government in the joint task of keeping law and order, collecting taxes, and so on.

I'm in favor of further democratization of the traditional rulers, but also in finding roles for them that make them positive contributors to the process of economic, social and political development. The moment they are given explicitly political roles and identified with one or the other of the two political parties, things will become very divisive. Having said that, I am willing to admit that there are contradictions along the road to constitutionalism. A lot of thinking still has to go into this, because there are inherent contradictions. I myself am almost an embodiment of that contradiction because my father is a traditionalist who is descended from a theocratic ruler, but my life experience has been in the realm of modern, secularized Nigeria. My own attitude is to believe that it is possible to develop some way of handling the contradictions.

QUESTION: I've gathered that one of the big problems is the strength of the fundamentalists in the northern region. I'd like to know more about those northern Muslims. Are they predominantly Shiite or Sunni, and which sect is more fundamentalist? Is there a large Muslim group which is opposed to the fundamentalists in the north?

PROFESSOR GAMBARI: Yes, the classic divisions between the Sunnis and Shiites exist and the Shiites are, by and large, the fundamentalists. Now almost 98 percent of the Muslims in the north are Sunnis. So if you look at numbers alone, you conclude that there is hardly a threat; there are very few Shiite Muslims in Nigeria. Many of these fundamentalists have gone to study and get some training in Iran. Fundamentalists are to be found among students and young people, who have come back to Nigeria from Iran. But numbers alone do not tell the whole story. Many of the fundamentalists sects, which are small in number compared to the total Muslim population, are very strong in their faith. They have almost the same fanaticism as young kids who go to die for Khomeini in the Iran-Iraq war because they believe that they are going to go to Heaven for fighting and dying in a just war. A growing pool of unemployed young people, particularly in the urban areas, and political leadership which does everything but live up to the ideal of fair and honest government makes for a very fertile environment for the growth of fundamentalism. They pose a challenge to the authority of the Sunnis and even the Nigerian states. For example, the situation allows the fundamentalist leader to say, "Well, you guys are in a serious, moral, social, economic and political crisis; therefore the only solution is for us to go back to the Sharia [Islamic law]," and sound appealing. That poses a number of problems, because not only is the South predominantly non-

Muslim, but in the western part of Nigeria you have families where the father is a Muslim and the son a Christian. The call for a revival of the Sharia, is thus an extremely divisive issue; it touches a lot of raw nerves. Yet it is hard to argue that the Muslims should not be allowed to run their lives according to the dictates of their religion. If you did, though, it would undermine the authority of the state.

Islamic fundamentalism may not appear to be a big problem, but it is really a very revolutionary and divisive force in Nigeria. To answer your question directly: If you look at numbers, the fundamentalists' influence should be insignificant, but if you look at the advantage they can take of the climate of despair in the country and the fervor with which they preach their fundamentalism, then we have a problem.

COMMENT: I just finished reading a book by a man at Oregon State University named Glen Daily on Central American politics. His thesis roughly is that the Lockean pluralism of the United States will not work in Central America. I think he would be willing to extend it to the Third World generally. Daily says that one needs myths of solidarity rather than pluralism in the Third World and that constitutionalism won't work. What is needed is something like Machiavelli's economy of violence; that is to find somebody, whether he is a military figure or a Marxist, who can maintain a rough peace with a relative minimum of violence.

I'm somewhat troubled by this thesis. At the same time, the idea that the United States can just export U.S.-style democracy, as the Kissinger Commission seems to think, is a bit naive, at least in my view. Since Kissinger is supposed to be a political realist, I've always been a bit disturbed by that. That does seem inappropriate, doesn't it? So where are we going, what direction can Nigeria go, given these two unacceptable theses?

PROFESSOR GAMBARI: That's a very interesting question. First, as I tried to show, an authoritarian model in which a ruler pulls everybody together by using violence, has never worked in Nigeria. I hope it never will work because it violates the temperament of the Nigerian people, which is to have some kind of unity while preserving their vast diversity; they value their pluralism; they value their free enterprise, and they value their democratic spirit. That's why all the military regimes we've had have not been able to rule as a simple military government; they always take civilians in as part of the government. Second, any government will have to cooperate with the bureaucracy, the traditional rulers, the intelligentsia and the media, which is another reason why pure authoritarianism cannot work for Nigeria.

Having said that, I don't want to give the impression that in some African countries such a system could not be imposed. I think that the smaller countries are perhaps more susceptible to rule by violent regimes or by authoritarian leaders. There was Idi Amin in Uganda; there was a madman ruling in Equatorial Guinea who was eventually assassinated because he was killing his own people for the slightest excuse; there was "Big Daddy" Bockafsa in the Central African Republic. All these countries have small populations and it may be easier to terrorize them, but Nigeria is too big, and too diverse to be long terrorized. Consent demands that there be a very clear limit on authority.

Of course, the problem is how we can achieve democracy in Nigeria given the conditions that prevail there. The wholesale swallowing of American constitutionalism or American political practice will not work; we must adopt those elements of Western constitutionalism that can best deal with our realities. I think I have mentioned some of the directions in which we have to go. The first is to maintain the secularity of the Nigerian state. That just has to be unless we want Nigeria to disintegrate, which is in no one's interest.

Secondly, a role has to be found for those people who exercise authority outside of the norm of constitutionalism. Somebody has suggested that we have, instead of a senate of elected representatives, another House similar to the British House of Lords, in which all our traditional rulers throughout the country would be members. One of them might be asked to be the honorific president of the country.

Perhaps these are not ideal structures, but it is a recognition that something has to be designed. The solution probably cannot come from a textbook, but must be an organic solution, one that emerges over time. The problem is that traditional rulers in Nigeria are local rulers; to give them national authority will cause problems because they are not national figures. At the same time, you cannot build a national constituency without the local grass roots; this requires a very important type of mobilization of the people. So while I certainly have no definitive answer to the question, I know what will not work in Nigeria: authoritarianism imposed by violence will not work. Wholesale adoption of western constitutional models without relevance to our society will not work. So we just have to find a third way; of course, the next attempt at democracy will be our third attempt and I hope it will not be, as you say in baseball, the third strike and out.

QUESTION: Perhaps the third try is the charm. Our own society had to go through a civil war after all. Somebody like Eric Vogelin would have said that every society has to have a civil theology or civil religion. I think he would have argued that simple secularism is not enough. In England, for example, there is some kind of creed—it's impalpable—which is a kind of religion. It's not Christianity or some other religion. It is just a basic belief. In the United States we often speak of the American creed. There are certain minimal principles that hold the society together, regardless of our differences. In our case these principles do rest upon the concept of the dignity of the person which ties into the idea of human rights. Civil religion can be either religiously-based or secularly-based, in case many people have no religious convictions. Do you think some sort of civil religion would work?

PROFESSOR GAMBARI: I can't see my way that far or that clearly but we too fought a civil war and the purpose was to make Nigeria one. In other words, national unity is our only real vision; no matter how much we fight among ourselves, the option of pulling apart now is gone. We have to make Nigeria work.

Now, how do we do that? What are the symbols? That is a problem. We have no truly national symbols, and few national heroes, and it seems that we are unlikely to get these unless we go back to the roots once again.

NARRATOR: Even Abubakar or Azikiwe was not a national hero?

PROFESSOR GAMBARI: No, because unfortunately Sir Abubakar, the first prime minister was perceived as weak. He was a decent man, but he was weak at the time when strength was needed to keep Nigeria together. Azikiwe started very well; in fact, he used to be called "Zik of Africa." He was considered by some to be bigger than Nigeria; he was Zik of Africa. (He was our first civilian president.) But in the end, the political party which he headed became little more than the mouthpiece of the Ibos in the East. In a sense it degenerated.

The one closest to a hero was Murtala Muhammad, a military ruler who was assassinated; he was very popular. He is the only dead hero we have. People recall the time that he woke Nigeria up from its slumber domestically and also pursued foreign policies that gave stature and prestige to Nigeria and Africa in the world as a whole.

Developing traditional roots and searching for national heroes and a national creed will be challenging. But I think if it is done, one of the things that we need is unity, the perception that we are all Nigerians, irrespective of language or ethnicity, with a common destiny. The perception of Nigeria as the leader of Africa also helps our self-image, that when Nigeria moves Africa moves; if Nigeria is not well, Africa is not well. It gives the sense that Nigeria has a mission to perform in terms of uniting the black race and maintaining its dignity. But this mission cannot be accomplished unless we are united at home and out material and financial resources are adequate.

QUESTION: You talked about unity. Since power, authority and stability depend largely on control of the armed forces, I imagine Nigeria has a problem since the armed forces there are probably under-educated and therefore strongly loyal to their top commanders. By what methods are you going to get the armed forces to pledge their loyalty to an independent, constitutional government rather than the top military commanders?

PROFESSOR GAMBARI: That's a good point except that your assumption has to be modified. The Nigerian army until the civil war was one of the most cohesive and the most disciplined army on the African continent and perhaps the most nationalistic of the country's institutions. I think what spoiled it was the length of time that it stayed in government, thirteen years from 1966 to 1979, and again from 1984 perhaps to 1992. The Nigerian army has since then become something of a political party. In fact, I call them a privileged political party, that is, they take over the government almost at will, claim to correct political ills and return the country to civil rule. But the longer you stay in power, the more corrupt you may become. As Lord Acton says, power tends to corrupt and absolute power tends to corrupt absolutely. This is a cliche that is generally very true. The fact that the armed forces have become a political party in the sense of an alternative government means that factions have developed within it which has weakened their cohesion, their nationalism and their innocence.

I would say, though, and this may sound rather mischievous, that prospects for constitutionalism may be enhanced because the army has now become discredited as a political force. In other words, the military have been in power so long, and the country's problems have become so complicated, that the military rulers are no longer seen as saviors. And if they are not seen as the savior, the prospect for civilian or democratic rule may be strengthened. As long as they are seen as the savior who comes and keeps the civilians and elected officials from plundering the people, they may have legitimacy. When that perception is weakened, it may strengthen the rule of the civilians in the future. People may then feel better off sticking with the devils they know, the elected civilian authorities, than with the military rulers, who often come in and stay very long without being able to solve any major problems of the country.

QUESTION: The matter of finding a role for traditional, tribal rulers in a democratic constitutional system is extremely difficult, but yet a key to success, not only in Nigeria but in the rest of Africa. Have you heard of any plausible and detailed proposals about how this can be done? If so, I'd like to hear it.

The second thing I'm interested in is the problem of population growth in Nigeria, which we read and hear a lot about. It's obviously related to the prospects for raising the standard of living, and that's related to any long-term sense of legitimacy of any government that evolves there. I wonder if you have any suggestions as to how that problem can be dealt with.

PROFESSOR GAMBARI: Let me take the last point first, the population issue. This is quite a serious problem; I read somewhere about a month ago that according to projections, assuming a 3 percent annual population growth in Nigeria, the country's population by the year 2050 will be 470 million people. That will be the third largest country in the world in terms of population. India will overtake China, and become number one, followed by China and then Nigeria. Now in relation to available resources and the physical size of the country, that would create tremendous problems. As of now with 100 million people, the quality of life for the citizens is declining. The demand for social services is outstripping the capacity of the state to provide them. Therefore the legitimacy of any regime is going to be seriously challenged to the extent that it fails to fulfill the aspirations of the people and their expectations for social services. Yet population control is such difficult a task to undertake because first, we must have a credible census, to know how many Nigerians there are. Then we must move toward some kind of a population policy which is difficult because Nigeria is a country that is heavily Islamic and most Muslims don't look favorably on family planning. Still, the state has to come up with some population policy and some enforcement mechanism to guarantee the very survival of the state. I think that the present regime in Nigeria has moved further on that issue than most other governments have, which is to say they have acknowledged the problem. At the very least, Nigeria is soon going to have a population count. Secondly, it will have a population policy. While I don't think it is going to be very strict, it will be a step forward. To answer your question, some steps have been taken, though not nearly enough. The problem is going to grow worse if nothing is done to strengthen those tentative steps.

Regarding your first question about the traditional rulers, no detailed proposals have ever emerged; the process of constitution-making in Nigeria and many of other African countries is reserved for the educated elites. The educated elites don't want to deal with the problem of traditional authority, like my colleagues in the universities who even see me as some kind of an aberration. They say that I have sympathies towards the traditional elites because I am a product of one of them. The reason why most Nigerian leaders don't want to deal with the problem, is that traditional leaders are using religion and ethnic loyalty to compete with the state for legitimacy in the minds of ordinary people. Traditional leaders therefore are consumers, or potential consumers of the kind of allegiance that the elected politicians would like. Consequently, the educated elite and the political class are reluctant to recognize them and deal with them. In fact, some hot-headed people propose that the chiefs should be abolished, but to me that is dangerous. I think we have to come to terms with them. We haven't so far because the people who should do so have failed to do so for selfish reasons. I think traditional rulers themselves have to come up with some kind of proposals for their role and to be credible they have to deal with rotten eggs in their ranks.

NARRATOR: This has been one of the richest forums we've had. It reminds me of the experience some of us had when the contacts between the United States and independent Nigeria began. Then a feeling prevailed that scholars, who were not the best, should go to Ibadan and Lagos and other such places as visitors. One of them was James Meredith, who you remember helped desegregate the University of Mississippi. I've never forgotten the interesting reaction of some of the best scholars at Ibadan. They said, "Yes, he's a very fine man, but he's not very bright." That was a sobering lesson for Americans because it taught us that there were a great many very bright Nigerian scholars.

Many African scholars have gone on and done helpful things for their country, though problems remain, and the challenge is great. Yet if there are enough committed and intelligent people who, like Dr. Gambari plan to return to contribute to his country's new constitution, there may be some hope. Today we've had a clear indication of the immense talent that Dr. Gambari brings to the study of the problem of state building in Africa. We are very grateful to him.

American and Islamic Constitutionalism: Prospects for Positive Interaction*

ABDULLAH AN-NA'IM

NARRATOR: We have been discussing the relationship between the United States Constitution and other constitutions for a little over four months. It is quite appropriate that we should turn now to the subject of "American and Islamic Constitutionalism: Prospects for Positive Interaction."

Professor an-Na'im is in residence at the Woodrow Wilson Center in Washington, D.C., bringing together scholars, policy-makers, and leaders from a variety of countries. The process by which these people are chosen is very rigorous. They look at every element of somebody's history before they decide on an invitation. In that connection, Dr. an-Na'im is especially well qualified. He was trained at the University of Khartoum in the law; the study of law begins there at the college or university level. He moved directly from high school into university legal training. He completed that program with distinction, and then went on to Cambridge University in England and the University of Edinburgh where he received his doctorate. He has made criminal law procedures a major area of interest. This is an especially crucial and sensitive issue when it comes to the interaction of American and Islamic constitutionalism. Questions that can be raised about human rights issues in that regard are very, very important.

**Presented in a forum at the Miller Center on November 18, 1987.*

Dr. an-Na'im has taught law at the University of Khartoum since 1976. In 1985-86 he was visiting professor at UCLA School of Law. In 1981-82, Dr. an-Na'im was Fellow at the Human Rights Center directed by Professor Louis Henkin of Columbia University. If Louis Henkin and his colleagues give the same praise and tribute to the rest of the people that have been there, they must have a superstar group because that's where we first learned about him. They hold him in the very highest esteem.

All of us are grateful to you for making the trip here.

DR. NA'IM: Thank you very much. What I propose to do is to discuss what I perceive to be the prospects for positive interaction between Islamic constitutionalism and American constitutionalism and then hopefully have some discussion on questions that can serve to develop certain aspects of my presentation. I would like to start by responding to questions that may have arisen in the minds of many of you when you read the title, "Islamic Constitutionalism." Some of you may wonder, is there such a thing as Islamic constitutionalism? I'll say both no and yes. The no is intended to refer to the historical aspect, and the yes is intended to refer to the potential or the future aspect. As I will be explaining, there is a potential for Islamic constitutionalism, but, as of now, in terms of the historical version of Islamic law, one cannot say fairly and reasonably that there is a very well developed sense of Islamic constitutionalism.

I wouldn't presume to discuss American constitutionalism, especially in this town, but I would simply note that maybe it would be useful for our discussion to take into account perceptions of American constitutionalism from my perspective. I come from Sudan, a predominantly Muslim country with a very significant non-Muslim minority population. It is considered to be in the Middle Eastern tradition as well as in the African tradition. Our country is a bridge, we would like to think, between Arab, Islamic North Africa and non-Islamic, non-Arab sub-Saharan Africa. So we have a very wide variety of cultural traditions, languages and religions. From that perspective, I would say that we perceive American constitutionalism very positively in terms of its ability to provide its citizens with a high quality of life, especially in terms of civil and political right. However, we have some reservations about American foreign policy.

We feel that this American system of government or non-government or minimum government has been effective and very successful in its national context, but it does not seem to have accorded others the same degree of benefits which it claims for its own citizens. This is the main criticism that we would raise in terms of our sense that somehow American foreign policy does not seem to translate the values which are held dear by Americans for themselves to their dealings with other peoples.

What I would like to suggest to you is that our high regard for American constitutionalism is in its domestic success, and we hope to get your assistance, not in transplanting, but somehow in relating that experience and that achievement to our own national cultural context. In other words, we would like to have the benefits of a similar system, which is appropriate to our own tradition. This is what the gist of my remarks will address. The values that seem to have characterized the American system or American constitutionalism at some level or other of abstraction *can* be translated or transplanted elsewhere, but they have to be given cultural legitimacy in that particular context. Muslims cannot choose values on the basis of the fact that they have worked successfully in a country like the United States. They have to see them as something that is part of their own heritage and as part of their own tradition. Of course historically speaking, Islamic law is the heart of the Islamic tradition because of the identification of law with every aspect of public and private life. It is not really positive law as you understand it in the modern sense, but it is the way that the law of God, through the Qur'an and through the traditions of the Prophet, has been interpreted by Muslims in their public as well as their private lives. That system of law was developed about 100 to 200 years after the Prophet's death, drawing on the traditions of the Prophet and the text of the Qur'an itself.

For those who may not be aware of the dates here, the Prophet was born about A.D. 570, and he started to receive revelation, according to Muslim belief, when he was about forty years of age—that is, around 610. By 622, he established the first Islamic state, and by 632 he died. He was succeeded by a number of very close associates as his caliphs, or his successors, who continued the state of Medina, which was the first Islamic state. Islamic history continues for the next 500 or 600 years in terms of the Umayyad and then the Abbasside dynasties.

But the law was developed, as I said, about 100 to 200 years after the Prophet's death. So what is known as *Shari'a* is a legal system which was constructed by jurists at least 1,100 years ago. You couldn't identify what we understand today as constitutionalism in that context. Constitutionalism as we know it today existed nowhere at that time—not in Europe, not anywhere else. It is unfair to judge *Shari'a* by the same standards that Europe and the United States have developed over the last 200 years or so. However, to say that *Shari'a* was legitimate and valid in its own historical context is not to say that it is valid for modern application. In the first case, judging *Shari'a* by modern standards is unfair; in the second case, the demand by modern Muslim fundamentalists for the reapplication of *Shari'a* today in the same way that it was applied 1,100 years ago is also unfair and unrealistic.

What I am suggesting is that, on the one hand, Muslims are entitled to assert their right to self-determination and to do so through an Islamic identity—to think in terms of developing constitutionalism and their conceptions of self-determination, whether domestically or internationally, with an Islamic motivation and orientation. On the other hand, I think they are required in doing that, to relate to the achievements of other human civilizations. To accomplish this, they need the cooperation of other civilizations, such as yours, in having a positive attitude toward them.

What I seem to sense here in the United States is that there is a tendency to view the Islamic tradition in a very negative and stereotypical way. This view tends to dismiss the achievements of that civilization and its own historical experience; it also seems to undermine Muslim self-esteem and underestimate the strength of feeling that Muslims have regarding their right to assert an Islamic identity. It is not something that they hold to be negotiable or open to concessions. It is a religious obligation, which they feel very strongly, and they are trying to wrestle with ways of complying with that religious obligation while at the same time relating positively to other parts of the world.

What I would like to suggest is how you or American institutions, such as this esteemed institution, can contribute to the development of this positive relationship. I see it as a two-way process. On the one hand, American scholars should take Islam more seriously and more positively and deal with it out of genuine knowledge and sympathy to the predicament which is felt by its own adherents. They should not take stereotypes or the negative aspects—which seem to make the headlines more often than the positive ones—at face value but rather look at the underlying economic and social causes of tension and conflict and relate positively to the whole process. On the other hand, I think that Muslim scholars should also be encouraged to interact with American scholars and to study the American experience in its own context and develop ways to make it relevant and useful in the Muslim context.

I would like to end my introductory remarks by saying that unfortunately the more positive aspects of Islam do not make the headlines. This includes the efforts of genuine Muslim scholars to address the issues that you rightly perceive to be very obvious problems with the Islamic tradition in terms of constitutionalism, theories of penal or criminal law, and the application of so-called *hudud*, the harsh amputations and floggings. Muslim scholars have been working on these problems very silently and diligently in their own context, trying to change their own population's attitudes and sense of what is the appropriate Islamic law for today.

One of these scholars is a man by the name of Mahmoud Mohamed Taha, a Sudanese Muslim scholar who devised a very effective, coherent methodology for what he called the evolution of Islamic law—not simply reforming Islamic law within its own historical framework and techniques but evolving it to a different level altogether without losing its legitimacy and authenticity as Islamic law. I managed to translate his main book, *The Second Message of Islam*, which was published by Syracuse University Press in 1987. For those who look at this work, you can see how a Muslim scholar has addressed the issues in terms of human rights, minority and non-Muslim rights, and women's rights in ways which would achieve a reconciliation between human rights and Islamic laws, between modern international relations and Islamic law. I think this is the key because we cannot expect Muslims to opt for a totally secular answer. Although we cannot expect them to shed their commitment to Islamic law, we can expect them to be willing to consider another way of relating to that tradition. That's why it is important to appreciate their need for help in this area and to relate positively to their demands or expectations.

QUESTION: You spoke to some of us earlier in the day about *hudud* and the discussions and issues that they raise. For a group of this kind, the question that would be interesting is, what are they? What are their sources? What are the principal problems that confront their application when one gets into discussions of human rights in general? And finally, what good are they? Have they done anything to deter crime? Another question that you discussed earlier is, what are the generational attitudes toward *hudud*?

PROFESSOR AN-NA'IM: The *hudud* [singular, *hadd*], the five specified crimes which are described in the Qur'an itself (Islam's holy book) invariably require very specific punishment to be imposed whenever the requirements of those offenses have been satisfied. The five offenses include theft and highway robbery (or a form of rebellion). In a strict sense, these two offenses relate to property. There are two offenses that relate to sexual conduct: one is extramarital sexual relationships, and the other is false accusation of such relationships. So, to be proven to have had extramarital sexual relationships is an offense. At the same time, to accuse another of having committed that offense and then fail to prove it is a very harshly and specifically punishable crime. The final offense has to do with drinking alcohol. As a matter of law, it is not clear whether this last mentioned offense is one of the five specified offenses or whether it is punishable under a discretionary power; in other words, conduct which may, at the discretion of the ruler, be penalized or not penalized. But four offenses are established; the fifth is controversial.

I would accept the four offenses as being *hudud*, crimes for which there is specifically required punishment. All four of them have very high and precise requirements in terms of substantive law, that is, what constitutes theft; what constitutes highway robbery or rebellion; what constitutes extramarital fornication and false accusation of it.

The Qur'an itself specifies a very high level of proof for these offenses. For example, for extramarital sexual relationships, the offense must be proved by the testimony of four trustworthy and credible witnesses who can testify to the actual act of sexual intercourse. Nothing short of that would suffice. Just to show how seriously the offense is taken, if three witnesses testify to every detail regarding the offense and its actual commission, and the fourth one wavered or in any way was hesitant, then all four of them would be punished for the offense of false accusation of fornication.

So you can sense here that the offense is intended more for its psychological impact than for its practical application. As a matter of law, all these offenses are not intended for routine practical application. They are intended to make a moral statement rather than to be the routine, everyday law applied by the state.

When you come to the wider social and economic conditions which have to be satisfied before these offenses can be legitimately imposed, you will find that it is utterly impossible to apply them in practice today. In other words, as a matter of law and from a human rights point of view, one can see that the procedural and evidential obstacles to the legitimate application of these punishments are so great that we should not really be concerned with them in practice; they should not apply in practice. That is actually the most fruitful way of facing the problem. You cannot hope to tell Muslims to disregard the explicit terms of the Qur'an, but you can encourage them to observe the explicit texts of the Qur'an in terms of the requirements and the general conditions that should be obtained before the penalties are imposed.

Unfortunately, you will find that at least as a matter of recent practice, some Muslim governments have tended to apply the harshest possible interpretation of these offenses; they tended to start with the penal and the oppressive aspect of Islamic law when attempting to reintroduce it in countries that have not applied Islamic law in this area for some time. In Pakistan, Iran, and Sudan, the reapplication of Islamic law started with the *hudud* penalties. They minimize the legal requirements for their imposition and publicize their execution because for them it is a public relations exercise. They declare a commitment to Islam which is in fact actually the opposite; it portrays Islam in a very negative light and gives it the appearance of a harsh, senseless penal law. That penal law, however, is a very minute aspect of the law as a whole, and has very strict requirements which these regimes do not observe in practice.

People should distinguish between Islamic law and the various distorted ways in which that law has been manipulated. The countries which have adopted Islamic law recently like Pakistan, Sudan, and Iran, as well as traditional countries like Saudi Arabia, claim to be Islamic or to apply Islamic law. However, the very nature of the Saudi Arabian regime is inconsistent with Islamic law because there is no hereditary monarchy in Islamic law.

So these regimes tend to manipulate and to abuse Islamic values and Islamic sentiments to prolong their own power rather than make a genuine commitment to Islam.

NARRATOR: Could you just say one more word about the draconian nature of the penalties?

PROFESSOR AN-NA'IM: I was hoping to spare you the gruesome details. The punishments are very harsh. For theft, if the required social and economic conditions obtain—that is, if society provides for the basic material needs of all its members, and if there is no *shubha* or doubt regarding any of the general or the specific conditions of the offense—then the punishment will be carried out.

Assuming that all the general and specific requirements are satisfied and that there is no shadow of doubt whatsoever in the case of a particular individual, then for theft punishment involves the amputation of the right hand from the wrist. For rebellion/highway robbery—it has to be an act of robbery by violence causing bodily harm and involving a degree of rebellion—for that offense it is the amputation of the right wrist and the left foot. This offense actually has a gradational series of punishments, ranging from this type of cross amputation to crucifixion when the offense is coupled with murder. For extramarital sexual relationships, it is one hundred lashes. However, if the accused or the culprit is a married person, the punishment is stoning to death. For false accusation of fornication, that is, if the four witnesses in any way disagree on any detail in describing the participants and the fact that they have personally witnessed the act of sexual intercourse—just the fact that two persons were in bed naked together would not do—all four of them would be punished by eighty lashes each. That's for false accusation of fornication. These are the four offenses.

As a matter of law, I cannot see a way of explicitly abolishing them in principle because the Qur'an is quite clear in stating their necessity. As a matter of practice, I can see that they need never be applied. Only if all the requirements are satisfied, which is extremely difficult, can they be applied.

Here you may, just for cross-religious comparisons, consider Jewish law. Those who are familiar with Jewish law know that there are very definite offenses similar to these offenses and punishments. Jewish law imposes very similar punishments. Jewish scholars developed the procedural and evidential requirements to avoid having to enforce the laws in practice. I think the Jewish and Islamic traditions, by the way, are very similar. We have our own view that the Christian tradition should be the same, that the Christian tradition was intended to confirm the Jewish tradition and that every aspect of Jewish law is part of Christian law. I won't dwell on that but simply point out that from the Jewish tradition and the Islamic tradition, the method is to obstruct or to minimize the possibilities of enforcement. But because of the very clear divine authority for the offenses, there is no way to abolish them in principle.

QUESTION: Do you think that this acts as a deterrent to crime? Is there less crime there than in the United States?

PROFESSOR AN-NA'IM: There is no empirical evidence to support either position. No scientific, empirical research has been done to show whether and to what extent these punishments do act as deterrents or whether deterrence is actually the primary justification for punishment.

From an Islamic perspective that is not debatable. The principle of application of these punishments is not that they all should be deterrents. Because the law is not decided on utilitarian or on some other justification, there have not been serious efforts to assess whether there is deterrence. In other words, it doesn't follow that if there is insufficient deterrence or reform, then the offenses should be abolished. Perhaps because of the element of the imperative religious nature of the offenses, the question has not been viewed in terms of empirical evidence or research. But we do have the claims, of course, that they contribute to deterrence and to a lesser degree of criminality in those societies.

Now whether it is due to that or not, it is true statistically that our societies (and maybe almost all other societies as well) do not have as high a crime rate as you have here. But I personally believe that our traditional societies—in terms of social structures, economic relationships, family, and extra-legal social control—have so far been more successful, or maybe they have not reached a stage where they would have to face greater criminality. It is true that there is less crime, but I don't think it has anything to do with the deterrent value of these punishments.

QUESTION: Is there a distinction in the application of the law between youth and adults?

PROFESSOR AN-NA'IM: Once the age of legal responsibility has been reached, then technically speaking there is no difference in possible punishment between, for example, a fifteen-year-old person or a forty-year-old person. But in terms of the *shubha*, that is, the notion of doubt, it may be relevant; you may take the age of the person into consideration in terms of whether he had intended or fully appreciated the consequences of his action. However, if you assume that age cannot be legitimately taken into account as part of the notion of *shubha*, the punishment applies equally.

QUESTION: As I recall, Anwar Sadat reportedly expressed his opinion that Khomeini was not practicing the Islamic religion properly. Would you care to say to what extent he was justified in making that statement about Khomeini? What was it about Khomeini that wasn't in line with Islamic religion?

PROFESSOR AN-NA'IM: I would agree completely with that statement. I would say that Khomeini was as un-Islamic as any of the secular regimes in the region. In my view, Egypt or North African countries which abstain from enforcing *Shari'a*, Islamic law, are closer to the spirit of Islam than Khomeini's oppressive regime. I think Khomeini's Iran, Zia ul-Haq's Pakistan, and former President al-Nimeiry's Sudan have been extremely negative in terms of Islamic law and Islamic values. They have emphasized the most oppressive, most authoritarian, and most draconian aspects of the law out of context.

I would support the right of the Iranian people to self-determination in terms of their own religious belief, which is Shiite Islam. But what that self-determination requires is a process of gradual resocialization or re-Islamization to educate and to socialize the population in Islamic values before the law is applied. You cannot suddenly impose a legal system which has been absent for many centuries. That's why you have such a high frequency of application of the punishments in those contexts. The other conditions of the law are not satisfied, and the objective of the government actually is not to give full regard to the requirements but rather to rush into a highly-publicized imposition of punishments. That is the object of the exercise. It is to give the country an Islamic face or to give the regime a claim to Islamic legitimacy. So I would agree with Sadat's statement. I suspect that it was the sort of statement that he would have made.

However, I would like to add that Sadat himself was not faultless in this regard. He encouraged Islamic fundamentalism in his own country for some time, before his assassination, as a way of countering political opposition. Sadat was the first Egyptian president to introduce an article in the Egyptian Constitution that made *Shari'a*, or historic Islamic law, the main source of legislation in the country. This element is now seized upon by Egyptian fundamentalists to demand that the government carry out its commitment under the constitution to make *Shari'a* the law of the land. In order to compromise with the fundamentalists or to gain their support, Sadat introduced an element into Egyptian politics and the Egyptian Constitution which I think will prove very disruptive for Egypt in the future.

QUESTION: When we refer to American constitutionalism we are thinking in terms of a framework for government. Would Islamic constitutionalism be a framework for government that would apply to Sudan, Egypt, Jordan or Iraq?

PROFESSOR AN-NA'IM: Yes, I think that this form of government would apply to any Muslim country and also to any non-Muslim country because it is not that different in its vision from American constitutionalism. It bears on representative government, popular accountability, safeguards for minorities and individuals, and on the essence of constitutionalism, which, in my view, is effective limitation on the power of government. All these notions can, I think, be founded on Islamic principles as well as on secular or other objective, non-religious arguments.

But what I am saying is that it is best, in our context, to argue for constitutionalism from an Islamic perspective. To give it an Islamic orientation and Islamic justification is the only way you can hope to achieve national consensus on constitutionalism and thereby have it implemented in practice. If it is seen as a western, secular, and alien concept, there is no prospect for success. If it is seen as a legitimately Islamic concept which may have some similarities and some differences with the way it is implemented elsewhere, that's where it will be possible to anticipate success.

NARRATOR: What place, if any, does a written constitution have within any of these areas in Sudanese society or Islamic society generally?

PROFESSOR AN-NA'IM: Most Islamic societies were colonized by either French or British administrations over the last century and the first half of this century. When these new states came into independence, they inherited either a French or British legal system and constitution. In all of the countries of West Africa you will find the French model. In East Africa, in the Indian subcontinent, and in Malaysia you have the English model. However, in these cases you have a written constitution which was modeled on the English Constitution or the French Constitution. In these cases you will also find that immediately upon independence, there was always a rise in demand for Islamization or the application of Islamic law and a decline in commitment to the inherited colonial constitutions. I think this is precisely because the colonial constitution seemed to be lacking in legitimacy, to be alien, to be imposed by the colonial power. Nonetheless, we do have written constitutions throughout: in Sudan, West Africa, North Africa, the Indian subcontinent, and the Far East. However, in all these countries they have not been very successful. They remain a dead letter, by and large, and I think it is a crisis in legitimacy more than anything else.

QUESTION: At the beginning of your remarks you expressed some disappointment that the United States didn't do more to export its view of human rights. On this matter of cruel and unusual punishment, or any other value that is found in the Constitution, it seems to me that we often run the risk of getting into a great deal of trouble when we try to export these values. In an Islamic context, wouldn't it make the modernizers and reformers vulnerable to the accusation by fundamentalists that it was alien, that the reform was being pushed by U.S. imperialists?

PROFESSOR AN-NA'IM: I'm sorry if I came across as meaning that America should export her values. As a matter of fact, I meant to say that this should not be the case. It should not be a matter of transplanting or exporting or imposing.

QUESTION: What is it you would have us do?

PROFESSOR AN-NA'IM: You should support the indigenous elements which have that vision in their own culture, those working within the context of their own cultural tradition, those who have their own feet firmly established in their own soil and cultural ground and who are appreciative of and trying to work within their own cultural tradition. Give support to that cause and try not to transplant directly or impose or export your values. The question of cruel and unusual punishment is very much to the point in that it obviously involves a value judgment. What is cruel and unusual punishment? Is flogging necessarily a cruel and unusual punishment, or are long terms of imprisonment, as others would argue, cruel and unusual punishment? From an Islamic, penal point of view, I think a case can be made for the humane nature of flogging as opposed to imprisonment.

COMMENT: Maybe we could give them a choice.

PROFESSOR AN-NA'IM: Of course, flogging is a much more available option for a number of other offenses than the ones I specified, and it is not actually that painful. It is intended for its psychological more than its physical impact. When you look at the requirements of the law for flogging and the number of lashes to be imposed—they are actually very light strokes—it is mainly intended for humiliation and as an expression of social disapproval. In those terms, it may seem to be a more humane punishment than imprisonment with all the implications of institutionalization. Since it is punishment in either case, the question of which punishment is more effective in obtaining its objectives, whether it is deterrence or otherwise, is debatable. The point I'm making is that it may not necessarily be the case that flogging is cruel or unusual punishment; that judgment has to be made within the cultural context.

QUESTION: I won't debate that, but how do you avoid the problem that to the extent that you are effective in helping those indigenous groups, you make them vulnerable to the charge that they are under alien influence? You could even weaken the reform. How would we help them?

PROFESSOR AN-NA'IM: You don't help them through official government sponsorship, to start with. I think that identification with official American policy or official American interests is a "kiss of death" for any indigenous group. Constructive help should take other forms. American scholars should take a genuine interest in the problems from a very sympathetic, internal point of view. They should take Islam seriously, take the Muslims seriously—not just in terms of stereotypes. The work has to be done by Muslims working in their own tradition. They can appreciate support being given in the right way, not through obvious interventionist kinds of action but through long-term commitment to the solution of the problems that the tradition is facing.

For example, many Muslims do not appreciate the role of religion in American society or the role of religious values in American constitutionalism because the Constitution makes a very clear statement against the establishment of religion. This makes Muslims think that American constitutionalism is a purely secular phenomenon, and they have a very strong suspicion of secularism. If American scholars could show that religion does have a positive role to play and is part of American political values or constitutional values, this would help Muslims appreciate that American constitutionalism is not as secular as the Soviets' is. I think this is one way in which, through their own work and through interaction with American scholars, a bridge can be established whereby the values of your own constitutionalism can be seen to be religious values that can be appreciated by Muslims from a religious perspective.

QUESTION: Could you tell us a bit about the more tolerant and accommodating aspects of the Qur'an, such as the views about the people of the book, and so forth?

PROFESSOR AN-NA'IM: The Qur'an is a very difficult source to deal with because it has all sorts of apparently contradictory statements. It is primarily a religious text and not a legal text. Actually, out of over six thousand verses, the verses that have legal content are eighty to one hundred at the most. Thus, it is primarily a religious text attempting to establish certain religious ethics or moral values.

When the Muslims came to construct the legal system out of that book they tended to emphasize certain aspects of it. In the process of developing a consistent, coherent legal system, they adopted a process known as *naskh*, which is abrogation. That is, certain verses of the Qur'an were deemed to have been abrogated by other verses of the Qur'an. The tolerant verses were deemed to have been abrogated by the more restrictive, authoritarian verses. So instead of freedom of religion, which was the original principle or precept, you had the law being developed in terms of classifying the subjects of an Islamic state with reference to their religion. Instead of equality between the sexes, which was the original precept for which you find verses in the Qur'an, the texts which came to be emphasized were those which made women the wards of men and men the guardians of women.

Remember that we are talking about the eighth or ninth century; that's when Muslim scholars established or constructed the system. In that context they deemed that people must be classified in terms of their religion and gender, that non-Muslims should not be equal citizens of an Islamic state, and that women should not be equal citizens of an Islamic state. In that respect, of course, they were not exceptional at all. As a matter of fact, when you consider the public law of *Shari'a*, you will find that it compares favorably to American and English law up to the end of the nineteenth century and the beginning of this century in the scope of the rights granted to women and the guarantees given to non-Muslims. But by current standards, you will find that *Shari'a* is definitely failing.

In terms of *Shari'a*, the first class is Muslim men; the second class, Muslim women; the third class, people of the book, namely, Christians, Jews, and Sabi's. From the *Shari'a* point of view, non-believers are non-persons. But even believers i.e., people of the book, have guarantees of freedom of worship, security of personal property, and personal autonomy, which is the right to govern their personal affairs according to their own religious law or custom. However, people of the book do not have access to participation in the national public affairs of the Muslim state. That's according to *Shari'a.*

According to Mahmoud Mohamed Taha, for example, this is all subject to revision now because it was based on an emphasis on certain verses in the Qur'an and on the repeal or abrogation of other texts in the Qur'an. The process that he suggests is to reverse the abrogation done by the early jurists. It should be open to modern Muslim jurists to reverse the process now by abrogating what has been enacted and enacting what had previously been abrogated.

QUESTION: Is the Qur'an more tolerant and accommodating than *Shari'a*?

PROFESSOR AN-NA'IM: The Qur'an has both elements. It can be read and interpreted as supporting *Shari'a* or as more tolerant than *Shari'a.* It is simply a question of which verses are selected as legally operative and how we can reconcile that with other verse. *Shari'a* has been historically dominant in a way which was less tolerant than it might have been. I'm not arguing that it could have been otherwise in the eighth century, but now it can be.

COMMENT: Might I suggest that *Shari'a* has been interpreted in the past, in the ninth century, by Borks (constitutional conservatives), and now you want to interpret it by Kennedys (constitutional liberals).

PROFESSOR AN-NA'IM: As a very vague analogy this is true. To put it in American constitutional terms that you may understand, the original intent that we have to take into account is in two senses, and it is God's intent in both. We don't have the Founding Fathers; we don't have the Framers. We have God. He is our constitution, and He is our law. But I would say He had two intents: an immediate intent and a long-term, postponed intent. His immediate intent was *Shari'a*, and it was carried out. His postponed intent is the second message of Islam (as explained by Mahmoud Mohamed Taha, that is, to come as of now). If you argue in terms of real intent, scholars can argue that *Shari'a* was apparently the real intent, but we would like to think otherwise.

QUESTION: Because the Shiites are apparently very strong on the *Shari'a*, how can they advocate terrorism, which must go under the second intent?

PROFESSOR AN-NA'IM: Actually terrorism is not sanctioned at all by *Shari'a*, but there is some ambivalence regarding the rule of law. Again, we are talking about a legal system which was developed in the eighth or ninth century, and the idea that there should be a monopoly on the use of force by the state or by local authorities was not very clear. There are certain elements of *Shari'a* that seem to support a sense of self-help, which was logical in that historical context. But now this seems to be used as a moral justification for terrorism. They don't openly admit that what they are doing is terrorism, but morally, individually, they would see it as an aspect of *jihad*, which it is not. It does not satisfy the requirements of *jihad* because *jihad* can only be justified after a formal declaration of war and only for an armed combatant in open battle. Even though terrorism does not satisfy the requirements of *jihad*, they would justify it morally as a reaction to what they perceive to be an injustice that has been perpetrated on them for a very long time by Western powers and their local agents.

QUESTION: By killing non-Muslims, do they go to heaven? That's what we hear.

PROFESSOR AN-NA'IM: It is a distortion, I agree, but I am saying that it exists because of the ambivalence regarding the notion of the rule of law and the historical *Shari'a*. There is a chance to manipulate certain texts to justify direct violent action, but I don't accept the justification.

QUESTION: Could you describe your judicial system to us? Is there a judge and jury for these crimes? Also, are your courts very crowded? Our court system is very crowded. I would think that with such punishments you would not have a very crowded courtroom. Do you have many lawyers in your country? Finally, if people commit one of these crimes, what does your society do with them? Are they outcasts like criminals here who are not allowed to vote and who find it hard to get jobs? What happens to someone who has had a hand cut off?

NARRATOR: Then if you have any time left, so that her husband doesn't flog her, you might say what you said earlier about the role of physicians in this whole process.

PROFESSOR AN-NA'IM: Actually what we have in Sudan is a number of parallel legal systems. At one level you have the English common law. This is a formal, territorial legal system of courts applying very formal procedures along English common-law lines. It is not dissimilar to what you have here except that we don't have a jury. For the more serious offenses it is trial by a judge and two lay assessors who help the judge. The three of them constitute the court to determine both questions of fact and law. Instead of the jury system, which we deem to be too expensive and cumbersome to apply in our context, we have for the more serious offenses what we call the major court, constituted of three members. This is the formal legal system.

Since 1983, *Shari'a* offenses were introduced, but the official judiciary refused to apply them. That is, they didn't say openly that they would not apply these offenses, but they stalled and evaded without openly saying that they were not going to enforce those offenses. So the government of President al-Nimeiry, which introduced these laws in 1983, established a parallel judiciary system initially called emergency courts during a state of emergency. When he had to abolish the state of emergency he called these "emergency courts" the "prompt justice" court system. That was the system which gave out most of these punishments.

Since the overthrow of al-Nimeiry in 1985, none of these punishments have been carried out. Because the laws were not formally repealed, the courts sometimes are forced to pass judgment according to *hudud*. But when they did have to enforce or to pass judgment on those offenses, the executive would not carry it out. So we have not had any amputations since the overthrow of al-Nimeiry in 1985.

The more important component of our judicial system is the customary courts, which I think hear about 80 percent of disputes. They apply in the countryside where the majority of the population live. They are based on local custom and are very informal and effective.

We don't have that much formal litigation, not nearly as much as you have here. We do have a few lawyers, but not as many as you have here, of course. It is the informal, traditional means of mediation which is responsible, I think, for 80 or 85 percent of the total workload. The courts have a very, very small part to play.

I'm not sure if I've covered everything, except for the question about physicians, perhaps.

QUESTION: Also, what happens to the criminal?

PROFESSOR AN-NA'IM: Yes, there is a very strong stigma. About 100 people suffered from the punishment of amputation over a period of two years, from 1983 to 1985. Because the evidence or proof of their condition and punishment is obvious, of course, they can't hide it, and they suffer much more from the stigma and hostility. When you meet them on the street, you immediately know that they have been subject to that kind of punishment. On the other hand, there are those who have been attempting to rehabilitate and compensate criminals because they feel that these people have been wrongly judged, that they have suffered the punishment without the conditions being satisfied. They have set up an association in Sudan to support, rehabilitate, and to provide artificial limbs for people who have suffered amputation. So you have both elements, but the stigma is very strong especially within the general population because they take it on face value as a genuine application of Islamic law. If someone has satisfied the requirements of that punishment, he would be socially condemned.

The point about doctors is that, like the regular judiciary that refused to enforce laws by stalling and evading the issues, when the *hudud* punishments were imposed by the alternative judicial system, Sudanese doctors also refused to carry out the amputations. They said that their duty is to preserve life and limb and not to destroy it. The only Sudanese doctor who offered technical assistance in terms of instructing prison staff to carry out punishments was condemned by the profession and almost lost his medical degree and qualifications. There was a very strong movement to disqualify him, but that was a single doctor out of thousands of Sudanese doctors. The rest of the Sudanese doctors refused to enforce the amputations, so the government had to resort to using prison staff to carry out the punishments. Once they were carried out, the amputees were taken to hospitals where the doctors took care of them, but as medical treatment rather than mistreatment.

One point that I failed to address earlier is the existence of generational differences. Older people who are not accustomed to the application of Islamic law, because it has been suspended for a long time, find it more difficult to accept than some of the younger people who are more strongly motivated by fundamentalist sentiments. Our extreme, right-wing, fundamentalist types tend to be highly educated, very young people who see it as a question of their identity and an as assertion of their Islamic commitment. Older people are less fundamentalist than most, but not all, younger people actually. The strongest support for fundamentalism comes from the youngest and the most educated, and I think that is why it has to be addressed as a very serious problem, not only in Sudan but throughout the Muslim world.

QUESTION: How long have the doctors said that they wouldn't participate in the amputations? From day one?

PROFESSOR AN-NA'IM: Throughout, yes. They never carried out a single amputation in the two years during which the punishments were carried out more frequently. Not a single amputation was conducted by a Sudanese doctor.

NARRATOR: I'm sure all of you would agree that the best guarantee of positive interaction between American and

Islamic constitutionalism is Dr. an-Na'im himself. We seldom listen to as clear an expositor of a terribly difficult and complicated subject. Since he has found Virginia in its very best appearance and character, we hope that it won't be long before he comes back again. Thank you.

The Impact of U.S. Constitutionalism in Africa: A Gambia Case Study*

SULAYMAN S. NYANG

NARRATOR: It's always a sign that *the* University must be doing something right when one of its graduates achieves great distinction in his field. This is certainly the case with our next African scholar who received his Ph.D. from the University of Virginia in 1974. Today we especially want to give an opportunity to his former examiners to raise any question which there weren't time to raise when he received his Ph.D. A number of them are around this table.

Professor Sulayman Nyang is director of African Studies at Howard University. He came to the University of Virginia as a Thomas Jefferson scholar from the Hampton Institute. He went briefly to Howard but then entered the Gambian foreign service and was head of chancery and deputy head of mission in Saudi Arabia; he was also accredited to eight other countries, including Iran. He knew many Middle Eastern students here, including a Lebanese student, a Libyan student, and a number of others. After a period in the Gambian foreign service, Dr. Nyang returned to Howard University and has been a distinguished scholar there since then. He is the author of the book, *Islam, Christianity, and African Identity: History and Political Analysis in Contemporary Africa*, which compares especially the leadership roles of Leopold Senghor with his

Presented in a forum at the Miller Center on January 16, 1989.

emphasis on negritude and Kwame Nkrumah with his emphasis on pan-Africanism.

He has written numerous articles on Gambian politics, probably more than anyone alive. He has written also on Islam and politics. He has branched out in his writing to studies of Pakistan, and he has written one of the few existing studies of the Organization of the Islamic Conference. He has a recent chapter in a book on the politics of Islamic revivalism, and he has written on Saudi politics toward the Horn of Africa as well. He happens to be a good friend of Professor Ali A. Mazrui, and he made an interesting comment about him. Mazrui, in the eyes of the left in Africa, is looked upon as a CIA agent and an utter reactionary, which is interesting inasmuch as the critics of his television program, *The Africans*, in this country attacked it for being too liberal. So Mazrui must be doing something right inasmuch as he gets it from both sides.

The discussion today is a continuation of our discussion of African constitutionalism, and we are especially pleased that, out of his vast background of experience and knowledge, Professor Nyang would discuss the impact of U.S. Constitutionalism in Africa, a Gambian case study.

MR. NYANG: It's a pleasure to come home to U.Va. I have fond memories of these grounds, and I'm very flattered to have my professors in this room this afternoon.

When we talk about constitutionalism and the impact of the U.S. Constitution on African governments, we have to take several factors into account. The first is that the American Revolution was a major event in world history. It was significant on two grounds. One, it was quite unusual to be a republican at that particular juncture in world history. We take it for granted today, because most of us call ourselves republicans in terms of forms of government. The American Revolution brought into the world system a new day when one could aspire to a position of leadership, not because of his blood, but because he is chosen by his fellow citizens. It was a major development in world history, prior to which we had the divine rights of kings. Men were rulers simply because of their genealogy or simply because they felt that they deserved to rule. Of course, our philosophers and political thinkers justified this system and wrote treatises to rationalize it.

Secondly, the American revolution was significant because the Founding Fathers like Thomas Jefferson and others were much concerned about the balance between faith and reason in the creation of human governments. In the past governments had been based on faith. Hence, governments were grounded on a concept of transcendental order by which rulers were indeed selected by the Almighty. In the American case, the Founding Fathers were able to devise a new system which made mankind recognize that there is a need for balance between reason and faith in human governments.

Scientific progress and technological breakthroughs in the United States are indicative of the great changes in the country since the Revolution, but the Founding Fathers were able to construct a constitution which has been elastic enough to survive the new interpretations needed to accommodate the social changes in human society.

With this background, I will proceed to look at the manner in which the American Constitution has manifested itself in influencing African societies.

The African continent is very diverse; there are over one thousand ethnic groups and languages. It is very dangerous and unwise to make generalizations. However, one can make a few tentative generalizations based on the historical record or the contemporary record of Africa.

When we look at African political systems, at least two general characteristics come to mind. One is that almost all the African states as we know them now as members of the United Nations were once colonized. Ethiopia, of course, was not colonized as were Gambia and Nigeria, but even Ethiopia suffered a form of colonization from the Italians before these invaders were chased out by the British and other nations who were fighting against the fascists during the second World War. When we look at the African political landscape, we see that the political systems were virtually all the creatures of colonial masters. Thus, in terms of American political influence, one can see that there is a fundamental difference between the American constitutional record and the course of political development in Africa.

When Max Weber defined political systems, he of course talked about charismatic leadership and rational/legal and patrimonial systems. When you look at the African reality, you find that the precolonial governments that existed were based on patrimonial thinking and patrimonial configurations. Tradition governed the manner in which the political process was carried out.

With the arrival of colonialism, the Africans were then subjected to an authoritarian form of rule. Governments were created which were not accountable to the Africans, because of the might of the colonial powers. Rules which were formulated by colonialists affected the manner in which resources were allocated, spelled the rights of the individual, and governed the interaction between the individual and others in society. The colonial period provided few similarities with the American constitutional process. One could say that the colonial period was authoritarian; the colonial period did not necessarily create any kind of parallel constitutional development which Americans can see as a mirror image of what transpired here.

The only context in which Americans can see any similarities between what transpired in colonized Africa and in America is to look at pre-independent America. Both the English-speaking African states and the United States did go through a British colonial experience. Thus, the manner in which legislation was carried out in pre-revolutionary America was very much echoed in the African experience. There is a parallel, then, in terms of being members of a community of colonized people.

Now, if we want to look at the post-revolutionary America and the manner in which it has influenced African societies, one should start with a close look at the postcolonial constitutions. In that way we can see to what extent these constitutions show awareness of the American experience on the part of African statesmen.

When you look at the African reality, you have to understand that Africans come from different countries with different colonial backgrounds and different cultural milieu. This naturally affects the process of constitution-making and constitution-building. After independence many of the African leaders were very much preoccupied with shaping political systems that were not only pluralistic, but at the same time unified to the point that ethnic division did not interfere with the political process so much as to undermine economic development. This was the dream.

Many of these African countries inherited the Westminster parliamentary model of government. The Westminster model provided a second stage in the constitutional development of African societies that were colonized by the British. Of course, one can identify a different pattern of constitutional development in the French-speaking countries. The same thing can be done for the Portuguese territories.

Since the Gambia falls under the category of English-speaking African states, I shall focus on the English-speaking countries. The pattern that has emerged since independence in small Anglophone countries like Gambia, Botswana, and Lesotho has been a constitutional replication, to some degree, of what transpired either in England or in America. In other Anglophone countries like Nigeria—and I believe Dr. Gambari discussed the Nigerian experience—there has been a military experience. The constitutional process in the case of Nigeria has been interfered with by the intrusion of the military in the political development of that society. It is against this background of diverse experiences and differential rates of constitutional development, then, that one can look at the Gambia in perspective.

When you look at the Gambian political system, you find that the Gambia is a classic example of a colonized ministate. In many respects it can fit the description of Aristotelian polity if the political process is carefully monitored by the leadership and if you have an enlightened leadership at the top. They must be in a position to create a political system in which all the attributes of a constitutional democracy are reflected in the political process.

Also, in the case of the Gambia you have an agrarian system. There was a preference for agrarian polities on the part of Aristotle, because he felt that maybe the best political system would be the one built on agriculture. The majority of the Gambians are agricultural people, and in that respect there is proximity to the ideal of the Aristotelian dream of the *politeia*.

However, the reality of the Gambian political system belies some of these expectations. One is the fact that in Gambia you have ethnic diversity. As a result the Gambian political leaders who moved the country towards independence were not only faced with an autocratic colonial system, but they were also challenged to deal with competition among the ethnic groups in the society. Therefore in the postcolonial period there was an attempt on the part of the leadership to create a political system that would reflect the national aspirations of the people and at the same time allow the opposition groups to register their presence and their disagreements with the policies of the government.

The British colonial authorities introduced constitutional government, limited though it was, in the colonial period as early as 1843. At that time selective representation was brought about, and in this sense there are parallels with the American prerevolutionary experience, in which certain categories or certain social classes were allowed to participate in the political process. If we are looking for American elements in the Gambian constitutional experience, we might very well pick out these building blocks that were quarried from the same place as those building blocks in the prerevolutionary American constitutional development.

From 1843 until 1965, when Gambia became independent from Britain, a number of constitutions were developed by the British. These reflected the state of political development in the society and the effects of social mobilization in the Gambian society. The pattern of development can be characterized by looking at the franchise. At the beginning those monied classes in the urban areas of the Gambia were allowed to participate in the political process, even though the governor was the virtual autocrat. He dictated the terms of political activity, and the colonial officers exercised hegemony over political life. This was the same thing that happened in Virginia at the time when Patrick Henry and others were saying, "Give me Liberty or give me death." At a later stage in Gambia, the British introduced a provision in the Constitution which says that people who own property—"rate payers," those who pay the rates to the local colonial government—are the only ones qualified to be put on the rolls. If you don't pay your tax, you are not eligible; in this case the constitutional right to participate in the political process was determined by your ability to pay the rates tax. Of course, this created a democratic aristocracy of a sort; there was an aristocracy of the rate-payers, who were allowed by the colonial government to participate in the political process. There are echoes of this in the American experience.

With the coming of independence in 1965, the Gambian leaders, who had been agitating for independence, felt that the new constitution that was to be agreed upon at Lancaster House should reflect the political ambition and the dreams of the Gambian people. Accordingly, the product of their negotiations with the British Colonial officers at Lancaster House was the Independence Constitution of 1965. A careful examination of this Independence Constitution of 1965 will reveal elements of the American experience. The Gambian Constitution has many provisions similar to those in the U.S. Constitution. The American experience offered a government which provided for a Bill of Rights, a supreme leader selected on the basis of popular vote, representative government (which was very much an American contribution to political practice), and freedom of religion. This last concept is very critical to Gambia, even though the majority of Gambians are Muslims, because there is a sizeable Christian minority and of course other religious groups as well. The provision of religious freedom in the Gambian Constitution of 1965 echoes the Virginia Constitution which Jefferson wrote, with its statute for religious liberties. Then, of course, the American Constitution also talks about the separation of church and state.

Also very much like the American pattern, the separation of church and state in the Gambia does not preclude the appreciation of the faith of the majority. This is quite evident when the president of Gambia or the prime minister takes the oath of office; he takes the oath of office putting his right hand on the holy book. Some may see this as a contradiction with regard to the separation of church and state, but I think it is a tradition that is not written into the constitution of Gambia. It's not in the United States Constitution either, but it is the custom that has been established in America. Of course, it was also done by the British kings, whose traditions are also incorporated into the political rituals of the Gambia. In this case, then, American customs and practices with regard to the assumption of political power have been adopted in the Gambia.

The other point to be borne in mind is that in the Gambia Constitution of 1965 there are guarantees for the freedom of assembly, freedom of speech, freedom of movement and the protection of the dignity of the person. All these are virtual plagiarisms of the American Constitution by all the other African constitutions. By 1960 it was clear that in many respects the American experience had proven to be a very meaningful contribution to African political development, and parts of the American concepts of government were found desirable enough to be accepted. A British constitutional historian may take issue with me by claiming that the constitutions were more an imitation of the British than American. But here I am willing to go part of the way with Gladstone, who compares the American Constitution with the British Constitution by saying that the American Constitution was created, formulated and written by men, who in their own way tried to live up to its ideals. The British Constitution, by contrast, was never written but simply evolved through practice over time.

The Gambian Constitution of 1965 reflects many of the same liberties that were aspired to by Americans and have been realized in the two centuries of constitutional development. When compared with the Americans, I would say the Gambians behaved in a similar way in their attempt to build democratic constitutionalism at the aspirational stage. Gambians have a constitutive ideal; democracy as a constitutive ideal exists in Gambia, and it is only history that will prove whether the Gambian experiment succeeds or not. The Americans have two hundred years to look back on and they can say, "Well, our ancestors faced their trials and tribulations, but they were able to work out a deal among themselves." Indeed, the politics of compromise and bargaining has yielded good results, and we are the beneficiaries of that institutional and ideological formulation and development.

The Gambian leaders were able to develop a constitutional form of government which reflected the

American ideal when Gambia became a republic. In 1970 we witnessed the last stage in the development of Gambian constitutionalism. In that year the Gambian electorate was asked to vote on a new constitution. The difference between the 1965 constitution and the 1970 constitution was that in the latter the Gambian prime minister replaced the queen of England as the head of government.

In this case the Gambians have traveled the whole mile, as the Americans did, in the sense that they were now saying, "We want to be truly republican, and we do not want to have a monarch. Our leader is not going to be elected to be the emperor of the Gambians; he is being elected for a specific time, and he may only remain in office at our sufferance. If we decide to keep him until he dies in office, that is our choice; it is not his choice to be in office." This concept is a major contribution of American political thought. One can be a leader, an "imperial president," or even what people like Ali A. Mazrui would call a monarchial president in Africa, but you are still a monarch with a term of office. This is an invention from America. People like Hamilton, of course, would have liked George Washington to be a king, George I, but that idea obviously did not carry the day. I think the Gambians have traveled the same road that the Americans have been traveling, but whereas the Americans have had two hundred years, the Gambians have had only twenty-four years of constitutional development.

In the 1970 constitution the Gambians worked out a provision that they will live in a society which is pluralistic. Moreover, the constitution will determine who is elected for what particular term in office and when he is liable to be prosecuted or impeached by the judiciary. Gambian democracy recognizes the separation of church and state, the freedom of the individual, and the ability of men to agree among themselves on how political differences can be settled without resorting to violence. After all, the bottom line of constitutional development is really the use of reason in the resolution of conflict among men. Men are social creatures who are faced with the daily challenge of resolving conflicts over property, over the protection of person, and over space. These are the critical issues all human beings are faced with, and in the Gambian experience there is an attempt to make sure that the rule of law is respected.

There is one point which makes the Gambian experience different from the American experience. It is true that President Washington was a charismatic figure in the early history of the republic. However, there were many powerful men around him, men of substance and influence like Mr. Jefferson, and they used their intellect and all the talents that the Almighty gave them to make sure that a government of laws prevailed at the time. In the Gambian experience the constitutional experiment is potentially in jeopardy because one man, the current president of the country, has been the most dominating personality in the political process. Many political observers believe that constitutional rule really depends on him. Some of us are hoping that this is not the case and that there are a number of other Gambian politicians who are equally committed to democratic process. Should President Jawara depart from the scene, we hope that someone else who is equally capable and equally committed to the democratic process would take over the system and that democracy would prevail in Gambia.

What the president has been able to do in Gambia is to recognize the rights of the opposition, which is a critical step in achieving constitutional democracy. If you do not allow the opposition to register their grievances, chances are that the issues are not going to be fully discussed and the opinions of those in power will carry the day as decrees. By recognizing freedom of speech, right of assembly, etc., in the constitution, you create a fertile ground for opposition to any policy pursued by the government. If the principle of rationality is elevated to the status of determining what is right and what is wrong in the society, then the governors who committed errors yesterday will have the moral courage to admit failure tomorrow. That is only possible in a democratic society, because dictators will always try to hide their mistakes by insisting that they are right, and in doing so, many will lose their lives in trying to talk them into abandoning old policies. Fortunately, the Gambians find themselves in the situation of having pluralistic government.

When I talk about Gambia's constitutional development and the American impact on the African states, I should conclude by pointing out that the Gambian experiment is a rare experiment in Africa today. Very few African states have multi-party systems today, but the number is growing slowly. The Nigerians, for instance, are in the process of returning to civilian rule. They have been trying to build a political order but, as President Shagari pointed out, there are only two political parties in Nigeria: the military and the civilians. Unfortunately, the military has continued to hold power, and they don't go to the ballot box for electoral mandate.

We have seen in Africa military men who have followed what I call the "Nasserite model." They are military men who try to project themselves as legitimate rulers of society by "civilianizing" themselves. Somehow there is this belief that if I replace my khaki uniform with a coat and tie, I will automatically be a civilian politician and I will be legitimized by my dress. Of course, this is precisely what happened in Egypt, and the Nasserite model has been copied by people like Mobutu Sese Seko, who first establish political parties and then try to legitimize them. Constitutions are then written, and the leader will try to justify his rule by claiming that he has popular support and that the new constitution is based on a referendum or a plebiscite in which the majority of the electorate has voted in favor of his position. This is precisely what people like Mobutu Sese Seko in Zaire have done.

The Gambian model is also different from the experiment that is going on in Ghana today. In Ghana there is a military dictatorship that has tried since the 1981-82 period to legitimize itself by creating pockets of support throughout the society. Even though the leader, Jerry Rawlings, now claims to be building up a society where people can participate in the political process, and the Chief Justice has been elevated to the second highest position in the government, there is still room for doubt as to whether a constitutional democracy is really in the cards for Ghana.

The Ghanaian experience is very sad because Ghana was the first African country to become independent. When President Nkrumah of Ghana took over in Ghana, many

Americans were very optimistic, hoping that this graduate of an American university would be the George Washington of Ghana. Many of the political scientists were somehow sympathetic. Many felt that Nkrumah's charismatic leadership could be utilized to make sure that you had an institutional transfer of democracy. This British parliamentary democratic model would then be replicated in Ghana through Nkrumah's intervention as a charismatic leader. Of course, this did not happen, and a one-party state was established.

This leads me to the other model which is a rival to the Gambian constitutional democratic model. This is the existence in many parts of Africa of the one-party state which became dominant at the time of decolonization and became much more consolidated in the postcolonial period. In Anglophone African countries such as Tanzania, the presidency is patterned after the American presidency. In the French-speaking countries executive government has been very much patterned after Gaullist France, where the president is very much like what writers such as Leslie Lipson would consider constitutional monarchs or "presidential monarchs" of the European variety.

For example, Leopold Senghor of Senegal, who ruled that West African state for many years, followed a Gaullist pattern and created a one-party state. Then towards the end of his rule in 1980, he decided to open up the system to other parties. The interesting point here is that the man who was elected at one point in his political career to lead the country later decided to determine the number and ideological character of the opposition parties to be formed. In a democratic society you do not determine who should be a member of the opposition; that choice should be on an individual basis. Each person should decide whether you are a member of the opposition or not, and this is precisely what has happened in Senegal. The same thing is true in Ivory Coast.

From a comparative point of view, one can say that the democratic constitutional model which is being played out in Gambia and in Botswana are two exceptions on the African continent; their experience has not been duplicated in many other countries.

This observation brings me to my last topic, the question of size. Some people have argued that size does make a difference, and if you are going to have a democratic government where people participate, then the fewer the people, the better the chances for a democratic political order to emerge. Of course people like Aristotle taught that certain requirements were necessary in order to establish the *politeia*, which was the best kind of *polis*. In the case of Gambia, the population at the time of independence was very small, a quarter of a million. Now after twenty-five years it is almost three-quarters of a million, but the size is still manageable; the political leadership is able to travel throughout the country and to interact with the people. To some extent this enables the leadership to have contact with the people; the president has a "meet the farmers" program that enables him to do that. This would not be possible in a country like Nigeria with a hundred million people and that creates a problem.

In short, the size of the country most probably explains part of the success of the constitutional democratic experiment in the Gambia. The fact that people in Gambia are not as ethnic-conscious as in other parts of Africa is another factor, though that doesn't mean that ethnicity is not a factor in the life of the people. Still, the willingness to mix with people of other groups and the accessibility of the leaders to the general public together enable the Gambian leaders to govern and to experiment.

Another point, related to the question of size, is the manner in which the president and his coterie of associates run the country. How do they relate to the opposition groups? The Gambian experiment was almost aborted in 1981 when we had a *coup* attempt in July of 1981. At that time some elements, projecting themselves as Marxist-Leninists in a bizarre way, tried to take over the government, but they were crushed by the army of Senegal. We were worried that this sad episode in Gambian political development could likely undermine the constitutional process.

In any case the question of size becomes very important. Other Africans often tell us Gambians that our small size has everything to do with our success in democratic experiments, but they probably overestimate the impact of size. For example, America provides a contrast to the Gambia, because America has over 200 million people and is a continental state. If America can successfully experiment with representative democracy, there is no excuse for Africans from big countries like Zaire and Nigeria not to try the democratic process.

African critics would respond that the Founding Fathers of the United States were much more united and that they had a lot of things in common which do not exist among the African leaders of their multi-ethnic societies. Clearly this creates a problem. Thus size may still be a factor when diversity is involved, and if size is not a factor, the ability of the elites to interact and to agree on the rules of the game becomes very important.

In conclusion, the American impact in the field of constitution-making in Africa has come in two ways. First, it has come through the post-colonial political engineering of African leaders, who have tried to establish presidential republican governments and have incorporated in their constitutions some of the tried and true techniques of government in the United States. Secondly, it has come indirectly through the British, because the African constitutions of the British variety patterned on the Westminster model and the American Constitution have a common genealogy going back to Britain. The American Constitution itself reflects a continuity from the prerevolutionary period and at the same time an innovation.

The Americans brought into the political consciousness of mankind the possibility of having a government whose head is selected by his peers. The president is not a warlord who exercises rule and domination by virtue of might. In America, faith in the Almighty and in the belief that all men are created equal, which is asserted in the Declaration of Independence, is the philosophical justification for democracy. This is unlike the situation in George Orwell's *Animal Farm*, where some are "more equal" than others; that is a tactic to justify and legitimize monarchy. In the American experiment, monarchical principles were jettisoned and individual rights, including the selection of the presidents by his peers to assume the reigns of government, became enshrined.

Those African countries that are now traveling along the democratic constitutional path are very much guided by these American innovations. In the case of the Gambian experiment we do not have the physical size of the United States, nor the population of the United States, nor the economic wherewithal of the United States, but the citizens in that impoverished state are struggling under a democracy. Poor states must ask themselves whether they can have a democracy which involves the powerful and the powerless in terms of economic resources, and still have the rule of law and the maintenance of justice. Gambia has been struggling in that direction.

In conclusion, I would say that indeed the American Constitution has provided a lesson not only to the Africans, but to the world at large and that the Africans have benefited from the ideas of the American revolution. The process of constitution-building cannot be a replication of what has transpired in America, but the sources of inspiration can be found in America. The Gambians are experimenting with a democratic constitutional model, and they recognize the fact that unless the constitutional principle is homegrown, it will not last. A lesson from America is that a nation may be inspired by others, but in the end it is your successful adaptation of the borrowed theory that makes a difference. Thus if freedom is to prevail in Gambian society, the Gambians must "indigenize" and domesticate what is perceived to be borrowed theory.

NARRATOR: When one hears so lucid a presentation, one always wonders what is the interconnection between the oral tradition in Africa and the capacity to grapple with these problems. Who would like to ask the first question?

QUESTION: You gave us a number of general principles and theories of both U.S. constitutionalism and the situation as you see it in Gambia. I wonder if you would go back over the last twenty-five years in Gambia and give us a brief political history. Could you indicate some of the issues that have tested these principles or some of the events that have allowed President Jawara to implement these rules? Could you give us a little more concrete substance to support the theories that you've laid out so lucidly?

MR. NYANG: Since the attainment of independence in 1965 Gambia has successfully grappled with threats to democracy on its own, except for the July 1981 *coup* attempt which required external intervention. In 1965 there were two major political parties in the country—the ruling Peoples Progressive Party (PPP), and the United Party. These two political parties were divided along regional and ethnic lines, as was reflected in the leaders of the two different parties. At the time the polarization was serious, because the urban areas were controlled by the United Party, whose leader was the chief minister until 1962. That meant he was the leader of the government during the final colonial years, but he was defeated in the 1962 election supervised by the British, and Jawara took over the reins of power.

In 1964 one of Jawara's political opponents, who later was one of the leading politicians in the urban areas, bolted from the party and formed the Gambia Congress Party. Now there is a very interesting development with regard to the emergence of this political party. Mr. I. M. Garba Jahumpa is the name of this leader, and he was something of a Muslim fundamentalist if we might use that term retroactively. He had been telling the British since the 1950s that they were favoring the Christian minority and that the majority did not have access to government jobs. Consequently he created a political party out of the Gambian Muslim Society, a coalition of diverse Muslim associations in the urban areas. A test of separation of church and state was clearly on the horizon.

In 1964, Jahumpa bolted the ruling party, but he was defeated in the polls at the next election. He had neither a seat in parliament nor a ministerial position, because the government didn't give him any position. Thus, he decided to form a new party. Fortunately, between 1951, when he founded the Gambian Muslim Congress, and 1964, the society had undergone significant changes. It was no longer popularly acceptable for a politician to bring religion into politics. As the society moved towards independence, religion became less significant and ethnic identity or regional identity assumed greater significance. Thus, when he founded his new party in 1964, he had dropped the word "Muslim" out of his party's name. It was no longer the

Gambian Muslim Congress; it was then the Gambia Congress Party. This was a very important development, because the political leaders in the country made sure that religion was no longer used as a way of dividing the people, thereby jeopardizing the normal political process and undermining the constitution of the country.

Another test case came up in 1972. The vice president of the Gambia, Mr. Sherif M. Dibba, was much compromised by his brother in the so-called "Butut Affair." (The Butut is the penny of Gambia; it is a coin with one-hundredth the value of the Dalasi, which is the Gambian currency.) Now it happens that the women of Senegal like to use Butut to make ornamentation. They wear them in various ways or they have chains made for themselves out of the coins. Unfortunately, the younger brother of the vice president was apprehended by the Senegalese authorities with bags of coins that he was trying to smuggle into the neighboring country to make a little money.

Of course, this was an embarrassment to the government. Here was the vice president's brother smuggling Gambian currency into the neighboring states. And of course the vice president was called in by the president and was fired. This created a good deal of protest, though, because Dibba had his own constituents. The government was based on a very delicate balancing of regional and ethnic groups, with Dibba representing one region. Thus, when this Butut affair broke out, the president was faced with a question of how to go about dealing with your vice president in an ethnic-conscious society. It happened that they both came from the same ethnic group, but they also belonged to different regions in the country. Even though they identified with each other when it came to alliance-making, they still fought for political power within the party.

Although this was a large problem, the president in the end was able to preempt any kind of challenge to his political rule that could have led to a constitutional crisis. Finally, he decided to take the matter to the party executive committee and then eventually to a party congress, which went along with his neutralization of the vice president. Of course, the vice president was then gradually eased out of party leadership, and he eventually left the party and formed an opposition party.

A process like this could not have happened in many other African countries. For instance, he almost certainly would have been jailed in Ghana under Nkrumah, and he would not have been allowed to form an opposition party. A preventive detention act would have been proclaimed by the president in most other African states. The vice president was allowed to form an opposition party, the National Convention Party, and he was able to operate freely without being challenged. This is something that would be very rare in many parts of the continent. Consider what happened to the vice president of Kenya in the 1970s, Odinga Odinga, when he challenged Jomo Kenyatta in a similar episode. Odinga was jailed and totally isolated. This happens in many other countries. In the Gambian case, the integrity of the constitution was maintained.

QUESTION: One has the impression that many of the present boundaries of African states were drawn by the colonial powers without real regard to ethnic divisions. In our constitutional history, we have been able to incorporate an expanding territory, though we had one major crisis leading to civil war when there was an attempt to divide the country. How permanent do you think the national borders of the states bordering Gambia are, and would any potential changes be the result of warfare? Are there any constitutional provisions for flexibility regarding borders?

MR. NYANG: That's a very good question. African leaders are being asked all the time, "When are the borders going to disappear?" Now, unfortunately, since independence the African leaders themselves have legitimized the borders through the Organization of African Unity, which carries a provision to the effect that borders are permanent. Article 2, Paragraph 7, of the United Nations is very much replicated in the OAU Charter, which talks about the sanctity of the domestic jurisdiction of states. That's one of the reasons why the Somalis have a lot of difficulties in Africa—because they are challenging the legitimacy of the colonial boundaries between themselves and the Kenyans and between themselves and the Ethiopians.

In the case of the recent efforts at confederation between Gambia and Senegal, the Gambians and the Senegalese are cousins. Historically, we are the same people, and we have the same ethnic composition. However, the colonial experience has created a new sense of identity among Gambians and Senegalese, especially the elites, who are the people who count in those matters, and the Gambians do not want to see the dissolution of Gambian sovereignty. Gambian elites will quickly remind you that they are not going to sacrifice their sovereignty on the altar of Senegambian solidarity. These "national feelings" are quite real, and they create a serious problem with regard to African unity. We have witnessed the coagulation of colonial boundaries, and I think people like Julius Nyerere, who at one time talks about pan-Africanism and the need for regional unity, recognize the sacrosanct nature of the colonial boundaries.

There is a paradox in African politics and in African societies. On one hand, the African intellectuals and leaders have advocated pan-Africanism, the dream of the unification of the whole continent. On the other hand, they are quite reluctant to dissolve any specific colonial boundaries so as to have piecemeal unity. For example, if Gambians and the Senegalese can form a union, this should serve as the basis for greater unity in the region, which would lead to the incorporation of other states. The Gambian leaders are very reluctant to do that. Since the *coup* attempt in 1981, the Gambians have signed a number of protocols and agreements with Senegal. These protocols were originally intended to bring the two countries together, yet except for security matters, the two countries are still far apart from each other.

QUESTION: You spoke of regionalism. Are the regional conflicts in the Gambia between the coastal area as against the up-river areas?

MR. NYANG: Yes, there has been regional strife within the Gambian and other states, but there has also been some cooperation among states in the various regions. The countries of West Africa have grouped themselves under the name of ECOWAS (the Economic Community of West African States). There is also SADCC, the Southern Africa Development and Coordination Conference. Likewise, the East African countries were grouped under the East African community, and several Central African countries cooperated with each other under French auspices. The African leaders have always been divided into three groups on the regional question. One group was the continental pan-Africanists, like Nkrumah, who wanted to see the whole continent united. Nkrumah was very much influenced by America, in that he felt that Africans should repeat the American experience by creating larger units, because African states were too small.

Secondly, there were the people like Nyerere who wanted to have a step by step approach to unity. Let us unite East Africa first, he thought, and then we can unite with our brothers in Central, Southern, and Western Africa. Finally there are the micro-nationalists, mainly in the bureaucracies of African governments, who don't want any unity. They have the cake in front of them, and they want to have the biggest slice. They are not too sure if their knife will reach the cake if it is expanded so that a regional government has control; they want to have it closer to home. This is exactly what is happening.

QUESTION: We have quite a bit of difficulty in determining what is really fundamental in American society in terms of the means of democracy. For instance, I lived in Westchester County, New York, and we had something called the "Town Club" where we had regular debates about issues. It was the town meeting pattern which they once had in New England. Virginia, by contrast, doesn't have the tradition of the town meeting. The new president of the University of Virginia has tried to pump life into the Senate Faculty as a democratic method, but those of you around the table remember that his predecessor was inclined not to assign as important a role for the Senate. However, one sometimes wonders how fundamental any of these *means* are compared with the *esprit*, the mystique of democracy, that underlies the different means. This must be true, I suppose, in Africa, too.

Aristotle talked about the ideal regime in theory and the best regime under the circumstances and many variations of that problem. I remember arguments in policy groups when people were just beginning to get interested in Africa, and those who advanced one argument saw the one-party regime evolving into democracy. This is the evolving one-party formula for which Nasser sought to provide a model. Nasser held out the prospect that when there was more stability and more growth, there would be a multi-party system. That was one hope we had about democracy in Africa.

The other path, towards which other people were leaning, was that the military is necessary in order to create order. If order doesn't exist in developing countries, you won't get justice and equality. They thought order had to precede justice and equality in all political societies. The other advantage to the military path over the one-party system, these people used to say, was that the military leaders were by and large more likely to have been trained in an American context. Therefore, they might be more willing to eventually abandon one-party rule or military rule, since they had absorbed some of these Western ideas in their military programs. These are old arguments that go back to the 1960s and the time of independence. I wonder what conclusions you would draw about them from the modern perspective?

MR. NYANG: Yes, in fact you summarized some of the literature that is current at this time. There is a reference group theory based on the experience in Ghana which has been trying to suggest that the military leaders would be very much inculcated with the Anglo-Saxon value of the military staying in the barracks and leaving the civilians to run governments. Unfortunately, this has not been vindicated by events in Africa. The military sees itself as a political player. This is precisely why Shagari would make that argument that there are two political parties in Nigeria, the military and the civilians. The military clearly sees itself as a player in the political process and in the case of Nigeria has now billed itself as king-makers, and the ones who are able to make the constitution become a reality.

There were also people like Rupert Emerson—whom I see in retrospect as an academic grandfather of a sort—who were very sympathetic to the Africans at the time of decolonization and who thought that the one-party state might evolve into a more democratic system. Political scientists were generally optimistic and hopeful about the prospects in the 1960s. I remember reading an article in the *British Journal of Sociology* by a British anthropologist, who tried to make the case for the one-party state by saying that it was very similar to the traditional African mode of governance.

The problem is that all institutions that are designed by men to restore justice and freedom are fragile. It is the men who run the institutions that make the difference. Democracy is not perfected by a constitution or by the institutions; it is protected by the collective effort of men over time. A system can always be subverted no matter how well you construct it. You can create checks and balances in the system, but if you have corrupt men manning the strategic centers of power, the system will collapse, and freedom and justice will disappear from the state. I think this is something we have to take into account. Institution-building is a long-term effort, and it is the collective effort of each generation that reinforces or tears down what we call the constitution.

The Africans cannot go any other way; it is the only way. There are people like Nyerere who felt that a one-party state would resolve the quest and would lead to the realization of a democratic order. Indeed, in their own way they have worked out a system whereby the rank and file of the party, including cabinet ministers, can be chased out of office. Yet they still have not worked out a system, in my view, whereby the presidency can be challenged, a system where an opposition leader can aspire to the presidency and then challenge successfully the incumbent. Should it happen that a person can challenge the incumbent and then replace him peacefully without any kind of military intervention or violence, then you have a system that works.

It is the men who make a difference. Nyerere reminded his fellow Africans of that by saying that democracy is a system which has faith in human nature.

Without that there is no democracy. If you don't have faith in human nature, faith that human beings can be morally sophisticated and morally responsible to govern according to the wishes of the electors, then you cannot have any kind of democratic system. I think the Africans are going to be faced with these questions. In their own way they will have to construct new institutions and develop new techniques that will reinforce and strengthen these principles.

NARRATOR: Every now and then the Department of Government gets arrogant so that when some younger scholar emerges, we think it's all due to the efforts of Professor Claude, Professor Fernbach, Professor Mosher and Professor Henry and others who are responsible. When we are honest, though, we know that is not true. We know that there are qualities that lead to the growth and development of a young scholar, such as we've witnessed today, that come from within. We're very pleased that you've come back to your home, and we hope you return many times in the future.

South Africa: A British Perspective*

SIR PATRICK MOBERLY

NARRATOR: The Miller Center is more dependent than we sometimes confess on good friends and people with long memories, and Mark Morford is both. He is a distinguished professor of classics at this university. About a year ago he was instrumental in arranging a discussion here with Professor Erich Gruen of the University of California when we were working on the subject of rhetoric, historical as well as contemporary. He also is responsible for our meeting today. It is entirely appropriate, therefore, that Professor Morford should introduce our speaker.

PROFESSOR MORFORD: Thank you, Mr. Thompson, ladies, and gentlemen. It is indeed a pleasure to introduce a friend of some forty-five years standing now. We were scholars who went to school together many long years ago, at Trinity College of Oxford University.

Sir Patrick Moberly had spent his entire career in the British Foreign Service, serving in Baghdad, Dakar and other distant parts before serving in London, where he was assistant undersecretary in charge of NATO affairs and defense. Following that responsibility, he became British ambassador to Israel in Tel Aviv for a number of years. His last tour of duty was as ambassador to Pretoria. He returned from South Africa this year and is now on appointment at the Center for International Affairs at Harvard University. It gives us great satisfaction that

**Presented in a forum at the Miller Center on November 30, 1987.*

we've been able to bring him over to this side of the water for this posting. I would like also to introduce Lady Moberly who is sitting beside her husband. Indeed it is pleasant to be able to welcome them both to Charlottesville and to the Miller Center. Without more ado, I'd like to present to you Sir Patrick Moberly.

SIR PATRICK: Mr. Thompson suggested I might set South Africa in the wider context of the superpower relationship. So I thought I'd start by talking about the wider setting of South Africa and then turn to the view from within South Africa itself. Then I should like to open the floor for discussion and welcome your questions and comments.

One of my predecessors spoke about the knife's edge on which any ambassador has to operate, meaning of course any British ambassador in South Africa. It is a tricky job and maybe the first thing I should establish is why South Africa matters to us, particularly the British. The first reason, obviously, is *apartheid.* We have to declare *apartheid* as an offense against humanity. It is unjustifiable, and what's more it is unworkable. Even the South African government has realized that it is unworkable, and so they've made some changes. They ought to be changing two things: one is the discrimination against black people and the other is the denial of political rights to black people. They've gone a little way on the discrimination side, but they haven't gone anywhere on the issue of political rights.

South Africa is unique because it is the only country in the world where racial discrimination is now enshrined in law and backed very strongly by all the operations of the state. What is needed is to see fundamental change arrived at peacefully, we hope, which will allow for a truly representative and nonracial system of government which the people of South Africa as a whole can accept. That's what we hope to see.

I said that we in Britain have particular reasons for taking an interest in South Africa, even more for historical reasons than is the case in this country, and it can be summed up under the headings of "people" and "trade". Let me first of all talk about the people connecting the two countries. We've done business with South Africa for a long time and many British people have gone to live in South Africa. Today many English families still have relations, distant ones at least, who are in South Africa. And there are approximately half a million people with a British passport inside South Africa and maybe nearly as many again who could get a British passport if they applied for it; they are entitled to it. So there are a lot of British people there, but visitors go both ways.

Trade between Britain and South Africa comes to something like $2.5 billion a year. British investment in South Africa is substantial; it is the biggest single, outside source of investments. It is a little less now than it used to be because, as in this country, some firms have pulled out, but the bulk still remain. Anyway, there are historical and contemporary reasons why people in Britain take a lot of interest in South Africa.

The third reason why South Africa matters is a strategic one. "Strategic" is an umbrella word and if you think what it encompasses the two most obvious items are, firstly, South Africa's position in relation to sea lanes and secondly, the minerals that come from South Africa.

Now, the first settlements at Cape Town did not come about because the Dutch thought it looked like a marvelous place to settle, but because it was on the way to the East Indies. South Africa has long remained a place on the way for ships. A lot fewer ships stop there today because there is just less shipping, and many of those that do go can go past South Africa without stopping. It has remained, however, a potentially important place in naval and global terms because of the shipping routes that go by it.

Everybody knows that gold and diamonds come from South Africa. In fact, 40 percent of South Africa's exports are in gold. Luckily gold and diamonds come from other places too, but there are some minerals like chrome, platinum, and others, the supply of which comes largely from South Africa. Therefore, the United States, Britain, and other European countries have an interest in maintaining access to South Africa.

I ought to mention two less obvious respects in which South Africa is strategically important. It is one of the land areas close to the South Pole. Antarctica is the largest remaining landmass which has not been used, occupied, or developed by people. In the future it may be valuable for its resources, and South Africa is definitely a window on that area.

The second point is that South Africa is capable of becoming a nuclear weapon state. Some people think that it actually has that capacity already. It has an enrichment facility which it developed, but of course it is not open to international inspection. It is possible that South Africa has gone a long way down the road to having its own nuclear weapons. If this were to be the case, it would be the first such state in Africa. In that respect, it is worth noting that both the United States and the Soviet Union would regret South Africa becoming a nuclear weapon state. This brings me to the last way in which South Africa is a strategic asset, namely, the fact that there is superpower rivalry.

I suppose it is true to say that neither for the United States nor for the Soviet Union is South Africa, or the whole of Southern Africa, of first degree interest. Nobody in the State Department has told me this, but I suppose it is about a second degree interest for the United States; and I guess for the Russians it is probably about a third degree interest. Europe, the Middle East, and the Far East are far more important to the Soviet Union than anything in South Africa or Southern Africa; and North Africa is more important to the Soviet Union than Southern Africa.

But there is a Soviet interest. The Russians, I think, have become more pragmatic in their dealings in Africa; they are opportunists; they exploit any opening they see; they have a number of clients they are prepared to back and help. But the American presence is more substantial; it is broader; it is more obvious; it is far deeper in terms of trade. It certainly seems from South Africa's vantage point that the Americans are there and the Russians are not. Each of the two superpowers has an interest in not allowing the other to become the dominant, political power in the area. There is no competition for hegemony but an attempt to deny hegemony to the rival.

The Russian presence and the Russian interest is absent in South Africa itself, but Russia is supporting two of the countries which neighbor South Africa: one is Angola and the other is Mozambique. Angola is the country where,

I suppose, there is the greatest potential for superpower confrontation. On the one side, there is the Angolan government, which is backed by Soviet advisers, Soviet weaponry, and Cuban troops, who, one supposes, are there consistent with Soviet wishes; and on the other side, there is Jonas Savimbi and his movement, the National Union for the Total Independence of Angola, or UNITA, which gets some American assistance; finally there are the South Africans. The American calculation must be that if Savimbi and UNITA manage to avoid being crushed by the government, in the end they'll have to sit around a table and work out some compromise in which everyone has a share in running Angola. That, I think, is an entirely laudable aim, but at the minute it is not actually happening and one has to question whether it will, in fact, happen.

The South Africans have an angle of their own to explain their backing of UNITA. The South Africans are interested because they are still running Namibia, which is one country further down the map, further south from Angola. And the people whom they are challenged by in Namibia are SWAPO (South West African People's Organization) which operates out of Angola. So the South Africans keep SWAPO at arm's length by operating in Angola. They certainly have been doing this for some time, on and off, and they've had to admit recently that there are South African troops operating in Angola again. It's the only country in the area in which the South Africans have had to admit that their forces are operating.

The other country where the Russians take a particular interest is Mozambique. It is tempting to think of Mozambique and Angola as being very similar in that they were both Portuguese colonies before independence; they both have had a civil war; they both have a Marxist government; and they both have Soviet advisers and Soviet help. I think, though, that one shouldn't take the comparison too far. For one thing, Mozambique is much closer to South Africa. Remember I'm looking at it now in part through South African eyes. Mozambique is an actual neighbor and has a common border with South Africa. Angola is miles away further up the map, or at least it feels miles away.

Mozambique really matters more to South Africa than Angola does. So far the South African government has been ambivalent as to what best suits them in Mozambique. Is it a settled regime and a prosperous country, or is it a completely unsettled country which poses no threat? I don't think they've made up their minds, but probably it is the former which is in the long-term interest of South Africa. As for the British, we want a confident, settled government in Mozambique with which the South Africans can cooperate. Hence, the Nkomati Accord of about three years ago in which South Africa and Mozambique tried to come to an understanding, though that looks as if it is only just holding. The Accord hasn't been denounced, but it hasn't come to anything either.

I've mentioned UNITA in Angola; in Mozambique, RENAMO (Mozambique National Resistance) is struggling against the government. I don't think the two movements are comparable in one important respect, namely, their viability. That is, you can imagine UNITA's leader sitting at the conference table with a program of his own and very clear ideas about how to run that country, but it is hard to imagine RENAMO playing a similar role. They seem to be a very effective guerilla movement, but they don't have a political program or an effective political leadership, and it is not clear what they would want or how they would operate. They don't seem to have the political organization to play a permanent part in running their country.

I think there is a third important difference, namely, that under Machel, and then under the present leader of Mozambique, Chissano, there has been a distinct move by that government away from depending on the Russians. They have made a strong bid for Western support: to the Americans, the British, the Germans, the French and others. This is something which can be encouraged because it does look genuine, and that indeed is why Britain, for one, has taken a leading role in trying to provide help of various kinds to Mozambique.

That's taken me rather around the area before getting to South Africa. So let's look at it from the South African government's angle for a minute. There are two points to make. One is that the South Africans do very clearly see their region as a whole. They don't think of themselves as just a country in a vacuum that is unaffected by what happens elsewhere. What is happening in the region as a whole matters very much to South Africa. The government has persuaded itself that it is facing what it calls "total onslaught," meaning a master plan worked out in Moscow to take over the whole region, and replace the whites in South Africa with a black government subservient to Moscow. It has led them not only to keep the African National Congress (ANC) at arm's length by prohibiting it in South Africa, but to lump the South African Communist party with the ANC. Undoubtedly, there is a lot of common membership at the top, but it is far from clear that this has been a wise tactic because the ANC is quite popular amongst the black people of South Africa. Because they are told that the Communist party is so close to the ANC, many blacks think the Communist party must be a good thing. It would have been more clever on the South African government's side if they'd let these people come out in the open. Thus the Communists would have had to compete against others and, I think, would have found they do not have tremendous support. The experience elsewhere in Africa suggests that black leaders who eventually lead an independent country are more interested in their own country and in its national identity than in gratitude to Moscow. The South Africans have probably done themselves no service by forcing people to think of the ANC and the Communist party as one organization.

The other reason why the surrounding areas dominate South African thinking is the government's obsession with the ANC as a terrorist organization threatening them. Neighboring countries are capable of providing support and bases from which the ANC can operate. Therefore, the South African government argues it is incumbent on them to make sure that these surrounding countries don't actually allow the ANC free run to attack South Africa.

The South Africans have used two methods to try to frighten their neighboring governments into withholding direct support to the ANC. One is military means. The South Africans have been across borders all too often in the past with raids, sometimes publicly admitted raids, sometimes deniable operations; sometimes the mere threat that they will do it has been enough. At any rate, they are prepared to use military means against their neighbors.

The second is economic leverage. The South Africans realize—and indeed they are right, and we fully accept that this is so—that the economies of those surrounding countries are very closely linked to the South African economy. Since South Africa has a strong economy relative to the others, the weaker neighbors are truly at the mercy of South Africa, if the South Africans put the screws on. Something like 70 to 80 percent of the external trade of some of these neighboring countries goes through South Africa; they are dependent upon the South Africans for lending them rolling stock for their railroads, as applies in Zimbabwe, or supplies of aviation fuel, as applies to Zambia, or electricity for their national grid in Mozambique. In the case of the Lesotho, which is entirely surrounded by South Africa, all the South Africans have to do is simply close the frontier and nothing can come into the Lesotho. Economic dependence gives South Africa enormously strong leverage over the governments of their neighbors. It is the consciousness of this fact that has led the British government to hold that one of the most useful things to do at this stage is to try and build up the economies of the surrounding states so that they are no longer so dependent upon the South Africans.

On the internal view of what is happening in South Africa, there is a great deal one could say. One of the main points is that the government says it is trying to change things. From outside it seems sometimes as if nothing has changed. I personally think that some things have changed, but they are not the central things; they are some of the discriminatory laws about where you can go and eat or stay or have a job, but the truly fundamental changes have still to come.

The government has settled into a policy of accompanying change with law and order, and it is desperately obvious to anyone who visits South Africa that there is a state of emergency. One can tell from all those terrible pictures one sees on television, or used to see, because part of the crackdown has been to make it well nigh impossible for journalists to report on what is going on. But the government does not apologize for that. In fact, they say the only way you can achieve change successfully is to do it in conditions where law and order are being maintained.

I think it is wrong to imagine either blacks or whites in South Africa as being static. Whites are shifting, blacks are shifting, and I sometimes think of it as two lines running more or less parallel. At the moment they simply are not converging. The question is whether they will converge, and I'm not sure that it is possible to say for certain, and one has to be doubtful, in fact, whether what is happening will enable the two lines to converge. Because, although I am confident that whites are moving, by and large, so are blacks. As whites gradually get to one position, blacks have left the point opposite of that and expect something more than they did earlier.

Black unrest is being bottled up and I think the blacks will become more desperate as time goes on. The whites are being pulled in two directions. The more obvious one is that they are becoming even more determined not to be pushed out. You had a white election earlier this year, and the people who made the biggest gains were the right wing. But there are some more hopeful signs within the Dutch Reformed Church. They now take the view, which is a remarkable change, that apartheid is actually a sin. It doesn't mean that they have a clear idea of how to get rid of it or what should take its place, but the theological basis for *apartheid* has been declared no longer applicable. Within the secret society, the Bruderbond, there are people at the top thinking in the new way. Within the universities, the Afrikaner universities, Stellenbosh in particular, there are people who are speaking in a way which couldn't have been imagined ten years ago. And even in politics there are a handful of Afrikaners who would go further than the government. But the bulk of the Afrikaners are still very unwilling to be rushed and to be dictated to from outside; they reject the idea that other people know better than they do how things should be worked out. This is really why the government has failed to get what they are offering, which is a round-table conference, or negotiation, or dialogue with representative black leaders. The government doesn't have the flexibility which would enable it to sit down with people like the ANC who undoubtedly have widespread black support. The government will only allow a few selected blacks to come to the table, and as a result none have, or at least none have until now.

I think I'll stop there. We can talk about the role of outside governments and how to influence what's going on, or any of the things which I've been discussing. I don't mind if the questions arc tough and pointed.

QUESTION: Have the whites drawn any lessons from developments in Zimbabwe, where the white minority regime was replaced by a black regime? If so, what lessons have they drawn from it?

SIR PATRICK: Yes, they have drawn lessons, but some whites in South Africa have drawn one lesson and others have drawn another. A smaller number of whites in South Africa can see that Zimbabwe, which has been independent for nearly ten years, has accommodated the whites rather well and that the country functions pretty well. They can see that even though it has a black government, whites are still welcome, and that some whites are returning. Shouldn't that be reassuring to whites? Unfortunately, more whites in South Africa would take the opposite view, a pessimistic view, and say, "The economy in Zimbabwe is worse than it was. They can't stop terrible atrocities happening from time to time. It is heading towards a one party state, and the one party will obviously be black. Things will get worse, and we don't want any of that here." And I'm afraid that taken as a whole, therefore, Zimbabwe is not seen as a promising precedent.

I think they are wrong because in fact they ought to be reassured but many of them are not.

QUESTION: I am curious about your opinion on divestment. As you know, a number of American corporations have pulled out of South Africa, having either sold their plants or closed them down. Do you think that does any good or is it bad for the Africans? American corporations will take the position that they are the most enlightened employers over there, and provide blacks with opportunities. Does divestment have any effect on the government in pushing it away from *apartheid*?

SIR PATRICK: Not much. I know this is a very sensitive issue, but I think that divestment hurts from the South African perspective. If you took your decisions purely in terms of how we can most usefully contribute to getting rid of *apartheid*, withdrawal from South Africa wouldn't contribute much. There are reasons at this end, however, which I think will prove stronger, so that companies simply can't stay. I'm sure the process of divestment will continue, because of all the pressures that have been generated outside South Africa. But has it made any difference? Very little. It hasn't made much economic difference because those businesses haven't simply closed down; they've been bought by South Africans, white South Africans in fact, who don't feel quite so conscientious about working conditions or contributing to the community at large. If you look at the record of divestment, it is not very good.

The package of sanctions imposed by the U.S. over a year ago, and similar packages imposed by London and the European community, has had the effect of stopping the earlier changes in their tracks. There has been no major reform I can think of since the main sanctions packages were introduced. On the contrary, what's happened in South Africa has been an even stricter state of emergency, even more people held without trial, and so on, and more curbs on the press. I don't think we can point to anything which says that firms withdrawing and government sanctions have got the South African government moving at last. I think that the actual story suggests the contrary.

COMMENT: Not from my point of view.

SIR PATRICK: It sounds as if I am totally against what has happened, which is not the case. Although in the case of firms I think they can contribute more by staying than by leaving, I do think that some measures taken by governments are worth doing because they don't force the government in South Africa to do things it doesn't want to do. They are a clear signal of how strongly we feel about it; I think the political signal is valuable. There is in fact a long list of British sanctions against South Africa. Mrs. Thatcher is against further sanctions of a rather undiscriminating sort, but we already apply a number of sanctions and the South Africans are in no doubt at all that we are serious when we say, "Get on." The difficulty is to find things which don't ruin South Africa but will move that process along towards getting rid of apartheid. It is very, very difficult to think of things which fit the bill.

QUESTION: May I take that question just a little further in the other direction? What is the danger of, and what could the West do, in a situation of polarization in South Africa due to sanctions? Are we pushing the white government further toward the right and the black ANC further toward the left so that large-scale violence becomes more rather than less likely?

SIR PATRICK: I didn't talk much about the deeply ingrained feeling amongst the Afrikaners that they aren't going to be pushed around, but it is in their history. One hundred fifty years ago they moved out of the Cape areas further north to escape from the British. They then made an attempt to establish their own, independent republics nearly one hundred years ago, and the British and the Afrikaners fought a war over it. The same mentality exists today: They are damned if they are going to be told what to do and be pushed around. Too much in the way of economic sanctions is likely to drive them initially into the "Laager," as these people call it. In other words, they will take up the position where they say, "We'd rather fight than give this up." It is at least possible, though nobody knows for certain, that all-out, comprehensive sanctions applied by everyone would have that effect. People who have the good of South Africa at heart, but perhaps haven't thought it through fully, have maintained that there are actually two choices. One is that things will simply get more and more violent and South Africa will go up in a tremendous explosion. That's one possible scenario. The other option is sanctions and their view is that if everyone applies very strong economic sanctions, South Africa will be pressured to change.

I think that's wrong. These two scenarios are not alternatives because it is entirely possible that very strong sanctions would lead to violence. It would ruin the economy, it would polarize black and white, and it would make violence an even more certain outcome or accelerate that outcome. So violence or sanctions are not two separate options.

There is a third route which is something like what's happening now: continued pressure and continued time for people in South Africa to change.

QUESTION: In the past, acting governments in South Africa had a majority of Anglo-Saxon or English-speaking people. What is the possibility of an opposition party formed by British descendants, who enlarge their base by bringing in more former Rhodesians, bringing in some more moderate blacks, and thereby become a majority government in South Africa?

SIR PATRICK: It's a nice thought but I'm afraid it's not likely. It's not realistic for two reasons. One is that amongst the whites the approximate balance is 60 percent Afrikaners and 40 percent English-speaking. So the Afrikaners are the majority among the whites, which is why they elected a government in 1948 which has been reconfirmed at every single election since. They couldn't face living in a country run by blacks, most of them are very right wing, and they support the present Afrikaner government, or people to the right of it. So I don't see an alternative white government taking over. It will be an Afrikaner government which has to change from within.

In fact, one point of which I have become convinced is that in the end the changes which matter in South Africa will come from within the country rather than being imposed or triggered from outside.

COMMENT: I would like to correct you on one small matter. In 1948 the National Party came to power with about 43 percent of the vote. This was typical because, as you know, the constituencies in South Africa have always been weighted since 1910 towards the rural districts. Hence the importance of the Afrikaners has not rested on their total vote so much as the distribution of the vote in the small rural constituencies. Until very, very recently, the National Party never commanded 50 percent of the vote. The only reason the National Party came into power in 1961 was because the vote was gerrymandered. No South Africans living abroad, and they amount to a large number, were permitted to vote. This has been the pattern. Many of us have blamed Prime Minister Smuts for not changing the balance of the population in the constituencies to a much more reasonable democratic pattern when it was still possible in 1939 and 1940. They did not do it.

SIR PATRICK: Well, there is something in that, but I don't myself think it is as simple as that. If, in 1948, the Afrikaner government had not quite got in, they would have the next time around.

COMMENT: They would not have been able to change the balance.

SIR PATRICK: Yes, the constituencies helped them, but it doesn't account for everything. It certainly doesn't today where in the last election the government did have a majority of the votes. Although they lost some of their old supporters in their own Afrikaner community to even more right wing parties, they got a lot of support from the English-speaking South Africans.

COMMENT: They do because there is no alternative. That seems rational at least, to the English-speakers at large. That is the primary problem. But in the past, under the South African party and the United Party up to 1948, you always had a large majority of the English-speaking population and you always had at least 10 percent of the Afrikaners, whom you might call the "anglicized" type, who voted with them.

SIR PATRICK: But I still wouldn't think it a realistic possibility that an opposition party amongst the whites could replace the present Afrikaner government.

COMMENT: I think with a correct districting policy it could. As an example, the Boer War is directly analogous to what is occurring now. What was happening then was that legitimate, white immigrants at that time were outnumbering the Transvaalers, and therefore the Transvaalers kept gerrymandering the vote. They required five years for citizenship, then ten years and thirty years, because they did not want "their country," as they called it, to be overcome or run by non-Afrikaners. That is precisely the situation today.

In my judgment, the only solution in South Africa is likely to be by violence. As Churchill said in the same context, "The Afrikaners seem to be either at your feet or at your throat."

SIR PATRICK: That is a sad conclusion, if you are right, that the only outcome is likely to be a violent one. I can only say that I hope not. You may be right, but I think our actions in the West should be such that we don't increase the chances of a violent solution; instead we should see what we can do to help it be a peaceful one. That explains some of the things we have done and some of the things we haven't done.

Perhaps I can just mention one case in which outside influence was tried. This was the Commonwealth Mission sent to South Africa in early 1986, which has been the only real attempt at outside mediation. It represents some progress because the South African government was persuaded against their initial feelings to allow that mission to come to South Africa at all. But left to themselves, the South African government would have said, "No thank you, we don't want these outsiders." They let the mission in, but once it got close to doing anything useful in terms of getting dialogue going between black and white, the South African government torpedoed it by staging raids against ANC targets in Zimbabwe and Zambia. This made it impossible for the Commonwealth Mission to go on.

My point in mentioning this is that there is a possible role for some kind of outside mediation, and I think we should bear that in mind. Still the primary moves must come from within South Africa. The assistance from outside could only be a small part of getting any real dialogue going. It can only build on foundations made by the South Africans themselves, white and black.

NARRATOR: Since you've sparked a little controversy, let me introduce a little more. As I understand it, the Reagan administration has been criticized on Mozambique, not from the left but rather from the right. This is due to the choice of an envoy who would have as one major responsibility improving the Western relationship with the government of Mozambique. Have you had political controversy of that kind within Britain about how Britain is to relate to Mozambique?

SIR PATRICK: No, but it was a little surprising at first when the British government began trying to give substantial economic help to a Marxist-led government in Mozambique. This goes back to the days when Machel, the Mozambiquan leader, was instrumental in getting the Rhodesia problem successfully negotiated at Lancaster House, leading to the independence of Zimbabwe. Machel showed himself a practical man who was able to compromise. When he subsequently indicated that he was uncomfortable being so dependent upon the Russians and would like to get some Western help, Mrs. Thatcher went out on a limb in saying, "This is something worth doing." And this help has continued under his successor, Chissano.

NARRATOR: She went public with that?

SIR PATRICK: She went public, and I think she was the first of the Western leaders to take this view, which is maybe not so popular here.

QUESTION: Do you think that the ANC's use of violence toward the white communities is going to be effective in changing the policy of the South African government?

SIR PATRICK: The South African government is adamant that it is not going to be moved by the ANC and especially not by the use of violence. But there is violence. White opinion is divided. Some whites think they have to talk to the ANC in the end, and think they might as well get to know them and explore things; a majority of whites are very distrustful. It is a fact that if a bomb goes off in a supermarket and white shoppers are killed, the whites' opinion that these are not the people whom they can deal with hardens even more. The pity is that the South African government, by prohibiting the ANC, has left the ANC no political role. The ANC is not allowed to operate, or have representatives within South Africa, so all they are left with is this wretched use of violence. One must blame the South African government for over-reacting and not allowing this political safety valve.

QUESTION: Is it practical to grant political equality to the blacks over the long term without the blacks taking over the government? And if they take over the government can the white lifestyle and the economy exist?

SIR PATRICK: I think that's the question which many whites ask themselves, and they can't clearly see the answer. That's why they are so unwilling to go down this slippery slope: They don't know where it is going to end. They imagine that they may be thrown out or the country will go to ruin under a black government. At the moment it would be possible for a compromise to be worked out which would allow whites to enjoy a decent life in South Africa. This happened in Zimbabwe where whites continue to farm, continue to be businessmen, and continue to be academics. But it wouldn't be as good for whites as now. White living standards would go down; the economy might not run as well; whites would have to get used to blacks being a majority and therefore being able to decide most things. It is still possible to work out that sort of deal. The tragedy is that if you wait five years, ten years, twenty years before the whites are prepared to say, "All right, we'll have to do it," it may then be too late because the blacks meanwhile will have moved on.

QUESTION: What do you think would be the effect if Nelson Mandela were released from jail?

SIR PATRICK: Nobody knows, and I'm sure the government has weighed this and tried to determine whether they can release Mandela. There was the release of one of the people with him, Mbeki, just recently, and it may be a test run. I think it is possible that Mandela will be released. There would be a great upsurge of enthusiasm in the black townships. That could run out of control, and that's when the government, the people, and the police chiefs will say, "We can't answer to what would happen in the black townships if Mandela were released and they all go wild." That's the government's worry. But what really matters is whether by releasing Mandela the government can then persuade Mandela and other blacks to come and talk to them at the conference table and start a process of real dialogue.

My own suspicion is that the government may mishandle this opening. They may release Mandela and say, "We've done what you've all been asking—you in the West and you blacks—we've released Mandela. Now come and talk to us." And the blacks will say, "No, that's not enough." Thus the tremendously valuable opportunity that is presented by releasing Mandela could be wasted. I would hope that if he is released, the government will have some more moves in mind, perhaps discussed very quietly with people on the black side in advance. This will take them beyond just releasing Mandela and offer enough to make it possible for blacks to come to the conference table. The blacks could then have the feeling that they have a fair chance of equal dialogue with government.

Those moves may involve allowing the ANC to operate again politically within South Africa, and certainly releasing a lot more of the people who are now either in prison or held without trial who could be part of any dialogue. So I think it is a very important step which could lead on to something, but won't in itself be enough. It could easily be thrown away by the government, unless they very carefully preplan what could follow after that in terms of movement towards dialogue.

QUESTION: I would like to bring you back to one of your earlier points regarding South African nuclear developments. Botha announced in September that South Africa would enter into negotiations leading toward ratification of the Nonproliferation Treaty. Is this a tactical measure to gain leverage in the West or are we on the verge of something very significant?

SIR PATRICK: I don't know. I left South Africa in July before this occurred, so I haven't had a chance to talk to anyone about it. One has to be rather cautious. It is a lot easier for them to say that they are prepared to talk about becoming a signatory to the Nonproliferation Treaty. Those talks could be stretched out over a long period with the South Africans raising conditions for joining. Until they actually sign it, I shan't be too optimistic because it would be a substantial step for them to sign that treaty. Nothing until now seems to make it likely that they would. They were prepared to talk about having international inspection of the enrichment facility, but that's been going on for quite a long time. Even that, which is a smaller step than signing the Nonproliferation Treaty, hasn't led to agreement.

QUESTION: What is the role of the unions since they were made legal in 1979? A few of them have advocated sanctions. Are they in a majority and what role do you think they would play?

SIR PATRICK: The role of the black trade unions particularly is very important because they are the one form of organized quasi-political activity which the government has allowed. In fact, that activity is becoming more political for the very reason that it is the only channel open for people to make political points for the blacks. I am sure that we will hear increasingly more about the role of black unions.

In retrospect, it may be a surprise that the government some years ago opened the way for black trade unions. I think the government nowadays must be rather regretful that there is this form of activity where blacks can take the lead, speak as equals, and become increasingly political. However, they are there. They've had one or two displays of strength which show that they are a force to be reckoned with. But the government has made life difficult, though not impossible, for the umbrella organizations of the unions to operate, particularly the biggest one, which is a kind of federation of black trade unions. The government detained some of its people, and mysteriously, its headquarters building had a bomb in the basement which destroyed the printing presses. I think that kind of harassment will go on. There will be constraints, difficulties, obstacles, and restrictions put on the trade unions, but they will probably not make it impossible for them to operate. So I do think they will be increasingly significant. We will probably see some very major challenges by the black trade unions to the big companies. There will certainly be a repeat of the mining strike of just a few weeks ago which the black trade unions didn't win, but didn't lose either. They will certainly come back and use their power.

I do think that the business of sanctions which you've just mentioned puts the black unions over a barrel because they represent their members, who have an interest in their jobs. They don't actually want to lose their jobs and be paid less because the economy is running down. They have no economic interest in sanctions; the very opposite is true. But because they are now political animals, they really have to take the view along with other people in the black community that sanctions would be a good thing, even though privately they can't truly want them.

NARRATOR: Mr. Burkett Miller urged that the Miller Center conduct discussions on any contemporary problem of national or international importance provided two ingredients were present: one, a speaker of wide and deep experience in the problem who could share his knowledge with the group; and two, a group who represented a broad cross section of opinion and outlooks on the problem. I think his wisdom has been borne out today. We are extremely grateful to Sir Patrick and Lady Moberly for joining us and to Professor Morford for making all of this possible.

The Debate on Democratization on Africa*

CRAWFORD YOUNG

NARRATOR: One of the most inspiring groups ever encountered in higher education was a handful of social scientists who went out to East and West Africa in the 1960s to take part in an educational enterprise in university development. James Coleman had a hand in identifying some of the more promising people. Some were chosen by those of us in New York. I still think of them as among the most remarkable people I've known. One of them now is vice president of the Rockefeller Foundation; another one, Michael Todaro, is the author of an economic development book that has nearly two thousand adoptions, including many in Europe. They went out into situations that were in one sense inspiring, but also had all kinds of difficulties, and they gave remarkable leadership at that time. Crawford Young was one of this group.

Professor Young was born in Philadelphia and grew up in Philadelphia and Washington; he received his Bachelor's degree from Michigan and his Ph.D. from Harvard. He taught from 1965 to 1966 at Makerere College, which we used to describe as "a little jewel of an educational institution" in Kampala, Uganda. It was devastated, we thought, by Idi Amin and his forces, but Crawford has just mentioned that it has been reconstituting itself. He was Dean of Social Sciences at Lubumbashi University in Zaire from 1973-75 and a Fulbright scholar in 1987-88 in Senegal,

**Presented in a forum at the Miller Center on May 11, 1989.*

so he has had a wide range of African experience. He has been professor and chair of political science, chair of the African Studies Program, chair of the faculty executive committee, and associate dean of the graduate school, all at the University of Wisconsin-Madison. He is the author of a number of much-discussed and highly-praised works in the field of African studies, among the most recent being *The Rise and Decline of the Zairian State* and *Ideology and Development in Africa.* He also is the author of *The Politics of Cultural Pluralism*, which has influenced much of African research. Finally, among other works, he has written *Politics in the Congo.*

He concludes our series on constitutionalism in Africa by taking a very broad approach to the topic. He goes beyond the merely constitutional subject in a narrow, legal sense, calling attention to social, economic, political, and cultural factors that are interwoven with constitutionalism.

PROFESSOR YOUNG: When Ken first contacted me some months ago about the possibility of coming here to make a presentation on the theme of constitutionalism in Africa, several recollections ran through my mind from previous sojourns in Africa. For instance, in the year 1966 there was in fact a new constitution in Uganda, and I recollect hearing a radio broadcast of a parliamentary session in which it was adopted. In that broadcast Prime Minister Obote, who was about to redesignate himself as president, announced to the deputies that they were called upon to vote in favor of this constitution, and that after the session, they would find the text of the constitution in their pigeonholes.

I also recalled an experience with constitutionalism in Zaire when the then and ever-yet President of Zaire, Mobutu Sese Seko, had just created by proclamation a new constitutional instrument. Under the terms of the new constitution, he named, in effect, all the members of the Council of Ministers, all the members of the Political Bureau of the party, all the members of the parliament, and all the members of the Supreme Court. Furthermore, he himself by constitutional right presided over all those bodies. I also remember about Zaire that the sayings and speeches of the President had constitutional force, and that jurists ran along behind him to create legal text from the new speeches that he made.

Interestingly, such disregard for real constitutionalism has been relatively rarer in Africa in the latter 1980s than in the 1960s and 1970s. Indeed, democracy itself has been more popular as a political model lately than at other times in Africa's past. The 1988 elections in Senegal, for instance, despite their flaws, are one recent example of this trend, which has been gaining ground throughout the continent. The Senegalese elections, with all their resulting strife, are symbolic of the struggle for democracy in Africa.

We might well ask ourselves why the preference for democracy might be stronger now than it has been in the past. There are a number of reasons, I think, one can adduce to explain this phenomenon. The world historical conjunctures, for one, play an important part. In the 1960s and 1970s, for instance, it was possible to discern in the world a trend in the politics of the third world towards more authoritarian forms of rule. I was among those who noted the trend, in *The Politics of Cultural Pluralism.* Perhaps that trend peaked with the emergency in India in the middle 1970s, a period when martial law was imposed. Clearly, that trend has reversed itself in the 1980s. We have seen, really for the first time in history, the full democratization of western Europe with the demise of the authoritarian systems in Spain and Portugal.

Once comparative politics paradigms for Latin America made reference to things like the "bureaucratic-authoritarian" state whose regional models were drawn from Argentina, Uruguay, Brazil, and Chile. Now, in the latter 1980s the very same scholars who created that paradigm are now preoccupied with transitions to democracy. From a point in time when democratic systems were the exception in Latin America, they are now the rule, the hope of the future. The states like Panama that stand out against this trend appear very much today as deviant exceptions. Elsewhere in the Third World we've seen once comfortably authoritarian NICs, rapidly industrializing countries like South Korea and Taiwan, being driven into opening their systems.

Finally, and perhaps most importantly, there are the extraordinary sets of events in the world of state socialism;

there are the tremendous changes in Hungary and Poland, not to mention the Soviet Union and China. In short, there is the sense of a trend in the world that is very different from the feeling we had ten or twenty years ago, and these kinds of feelings about new trends tend to spill over; they reverberate throughout our "planetary village" from one part of the world to the other. Only the Middle East stands out as an exception to this trend, with its tough military regimes such as Iraq and Syria, its patrimonial monarchies such as Saudi Arabia and the United Arab Emirates, Leninist states such as South Yemen, and theocracies such as Iran. In any other region there are democratic currents running which are impossible to ignore.

This in turn relates to a second factor, and that is the decline in the credibility of political doctrines that justify authoritarianism. Fascism, of course, was discredited by World War II, but Marxism-Leninism as a political formula and Leninism as an idea of state organization, were not at all discredited. Indeed, from 1919 to what the Soviets now call the "era of the stagnation," i.e., Brezhnev's period, almost everybody thought that the Soviet Union and China (until after the Cultural Revolution) at whatever human or political cost had discovered a formula for rapid economic transformation. Today few people believe that; that's a major change in the perceptions of the world.

In the comparative politics literature through the 1960s and into the 1970s, there was a set of arguments that took a very benign view of single-party systems and military formulas. Many of my colleagues and I participated in creating these arguments, in fact. While I share responsibility for justifying the single-party, I do disavow any connection with the body of theory that praised the *military regimes* for their national integrative potential or for their sense of purpose and purity of behavior in office. Nonetheless, there was such a body of literature in the 1960s which had real credibility. It was only after a decade or more of observing the performance of those kinds of systems that it became indisputable, on the basis of simple empirical evidence, that military and single-party regimes were not performing better in terms of development than other kinds of regimes. Indeed many, such as the

Philippines and Argentina, fared much worse under these kinds of regimes.

We find that even scholars who once might have believed in, for example, the socialist, single-party formula are now arguing a very different line. For example, a very influential African Marxist scholar, an excellent Kenyan political scientist named Peter Anyang' Nyong'o, wrote as follows in a book that appeared last year:

> The flowering of a bourgeois democratic republic therefore creates the objective conditions in which the oppressed classes can organize and prepare, over a long time perspective, for the emancipation from the rule of capital. That, indeed, will be the day when classes in bourgeois society will have been abolished and a completely new society, a communist one, will have been born. But that is in the future; as of now, the popular masses must struggle under concrete historical circumstances to create the conditions for the realization of that distant future, and that means making the best out of the bourgeois democratic republic.

Clearly this is a new kind of Marxist argument. The new thinking from all quarters has it that authoritarian formulas will not be able to deliver the promised goods, whatever one considers the promised goods to be.

A third factor of our present world historical moment is the indisputable trend towards liberalization of economies, whether it is done by choice or under duress. Liberalization has been by choice in many western countries, and under partial duress due to the pressure of international financial institutions in many African states. There is some historical interrelationship between statism in the political realm and statism in the economic realm. I don't want to be understood as exhuming a Hayek kind of argument here, pronouncing a rigid causal undeniably connection, but nonetheless there is some interaction. The inescapability of rolling back the state in its economic role around the world has been another factor that contributes to limiting the state's political role. Moreover, in highly statist political economies, such as those in most of Africa, economic liberalization can result in new economic categories, including classes and other economic forces that have a new degree of autonomy as groups. These groups are often in a stronger position to demand accountability on the part of the state, and space for themselves. This in turn plays an institutional role in a process of democratization.

A fourth factor I'd like to mention is the rise of a structured and organized human rights movement since 1945. I think this movement has been gaining momentum since the Helsinki Agreement of 1975. It is surprising how sensitive regimes are to the data that is generated by these human rights organizations. These organizations, such as Amnesty International, Human Rights Watch (which has just recently created its own "Africa Watch" section), etc., are places to whom opposition elements can run. Dissidents who believe themselves to be oppressed or mistreated can take their information to the organizations and hope for relief. This feeds back into the international human rights realm and creates pressures on the regime; the regimes can't wholly dismiss these kinds of things. While I wouldn't want to argue that Amnesty International or Human Rights Watch have a controlling effect, much less that Western states have consistent positions on human rights issues, human rights pressure is part of the dynamic that's entering the picture.

In short, there is a trend towards democracy and an aspiration for democratization of the states of Africa with a growing hold on many segments of society. I can speak not only from the experience of my stay in Senegal last year, but also from the opportunity to travel to some neighboring countries.

The question then arises that if we want democracy, what is it that we want? What is it that we want when we want democracy? George Orwell, as is often the case, has a very appropriately pungent quotation that I'd like to read to introduce this topic:

> In the case of a word like "democracy" not only is there no agreed definition, but the attempt to make one is resisted from all sides . . . The defenders of any kind of regime claim that it is a

> democracy, and fear that they might have to stop using the word if it were tied to any one meaning.

Indeed, this debate on democratization does have a certain negative backdrop. There are innumerable instances of the perversion of the term in the quest for legitimacy of authoritarian regimes of different descriptions. For instance, East European states in their most Stalinist forms used to call themselves "People's Democracies." One of Africa's more distinguished autocrats, Mobutu Sese Seko, frequently describes himself as a great democrat. Sêkou Tourê's party, which arguably had democratic mobilizational elements to it in the nationalist period, but which quickly took on an autocratic tone after independence, labeled itself Parti Democratique du Guineê. Under Tourè, Guinea was hardly a democratic state by any recognizable standard. With many perversions of the term, then, there is indeed need to ask ourselves: Can we distill a common essence to this notion? In fact, it is doubtful that we can get a common essence, but there are some themes that we might look at. Here we will come back to the real focus of this discussion.

Democracy is, in part, constitutionalism, though it is more as well. Historically, and especially in the rise of the modern Western state, constitutionalism arises out of a growing struggle on the part of civil society to constrain or limit control by the absolutist state, such as those constructed by centralizing monarchies in Europe. The doctrines of popular sovereignty, parliamentary supremacy, etc., are precisely a product of this struggle that extended over many decades, indeed even centuries. Constitutionalism has to do with making the state into a *rechtstaat*, an *ètat de droit*, a state that is governed by its own public law. This kind of state is accountable; it has elements of legislative control or a monitoring supervision of the executive. The administration of justice is autotomized through the judicial system, and so forth.

Besides being constitutionalism, democracy is also accountability and responsiveness. The notions of accountability and responsiveness lead us into the process elements of democracy. There is a necessity of rendering rulers answerable through electoral processes that include political competition, with these in turn including procedures that guarantee these processes—freedom of association, freedom of expression, and so forth.

Another theme that emerges in this debate is the one over democracy as personal liberty. Democracy among other things is related to some kind of shelter around the individual citizen that permits him to have a zone of autonomous behavior and to enjoy the array of prerogatives that we know as civil liberties.

Another important sense or meaning of democracy involves the idea of equality, that individuals should have equal valuation within the state. This "populist" dimension, if you will, of democracy is one that leads to evaluation of democracy by the outcomes of the social and economic policies that states pursue. There is a fascinating article in the latest *Comparative Politics* on "Concepts of Democracy Among the Brazilian Public." The survey shows a rather profound divergence of views amongst the Brazilian public between those whose central perception of democracy is process (elections, civil liberties, etc.) and those whose central perception is populism. The second group believes that democracy is something that produces more equitable returns for the popular sectors of society. My sense of the unfolding Brazilian electoral process is that it is precisely playing out that drama between these two different notions of what democratization in Brazil should be. Likewise, in Senegal in 1988, the young people who roamed the streets chanting "*Sopi*," which means "change" in the Wolof language, were essentially expressing a populist understanding of what democracy is.

Thus we have several rather different themes or components to democracy, that, as innumerable theorists on the subject of democracy have told us, are unequally represented in any particular regime. In the translation of democracy from a normative doctrine into an empirical formula for rule, the specific combination of these different components will necessarily be contingent upon historical, contextual, situational factors in the particular environment.

In Africa, the debate on democracy is drawing upon a universal discourse—they use that expression—but its text is within a very specifically African environment. It is shaped by the particular trajectories of the African state, which are not those of the European state, the Asian state, the Latin American state, or others. One particular part of the African context for democracy is this pervasive sense of crisis or impasse. That word "crisis" is encountered every place in Africa. It doesn't mean the same thing every place, because it's much more intense in some places than others. Senegal, for example, is by no means as dislocated as Zaire or Uganda. Nonetheless, everybody talks about the "crisis"; the vocabulary is the same, and some of its meanings are similar. Something is awry. The present cannot be indefinitely projected into the future; something has to give.

How then did one get to where one now is? Well, to unravel the specific trajectory of the African state, we need to begin with the singularly authoritarian legacy of the colonial state. While I cannot fully develop this argument, I would maintain that the African colonial state had, in the fulfillment of its vocation of domination in African society, constructed a more thoroughgoing kind of hegemonical authoritarianism than was the case in any other formally colonized regions. It was only at the very last minute, because nobody in the European capitals anticipated the speed that decolonization finally took, that there was a real effort to constitutionalize, to introduce democracy. And yet when it was introduced, it was made, in a certain respect, a ransom of independence; that is, nationalist forces had to legitimate their claims in most instances by securing electoral majorities under supervision of the withdrawing colonial authorities. This was not a constitutionalization of a state; it was a one-shot ransom of independence. Thus, the authoritarian legacy was embedded in the post-colonial state.

However, political management of the post-colonial state could not take place in the same way as in its colonial predecessor. Power, to be reproduced over time—the natural inclination of any ruler—had to be patrimonialized. Networks of clientage and offices as rewards came to be a seemingly inevitable part of the strategies designed by incumbents to preserve their positions in power. There was as well, because this system offered no institutional mechanisms for change or succession, either instability through *coups* or an ossification of power through the life-long presidency. All of these things, in turn, led over time to this phenomenon of exit, withdrawal, and disengagement of civil society from the state and the state economy.

This widespread disaffection with the state had a couple of major yardsticks. There was a temporal yardstick, for example. For an older generation, those who could remember the process of decolonization, there was, on the one hand, a recollection of perhaps the happiest part of the colonial period. They remembered the 1950s, which happened to be the only time during the whole colonial period when there was a rising standard of living. These people sometimes contrast that period with parts of the independence period, so that when you travel to places like Zaire, you hear older people talking with nostalgia about "*le temps der Belges*." That's a jarring kind of thing. They don't mean all the vexatious, oppressive aspects of the colonial system, but rather they mean a more predictable, stable existence when there was not hyper-inflation and when there were not shortages of all kinds of things.

The young generation has a different yardstick, and that is its perception of the future. The tragic perception of the future of this generation of teenagers is that there *is* no future for them. There are no jobs when you get out of the university or even secondary school; economies are contracting; structural adjustment, alas, is having not terribly visible, positive effects (though its immediate negative social consequences fall very heavily upon this generation). Thus the kinds of dramas that one saw in Dakar during 1988 or that one saw last October in Algiers are very much a generational thing having to do with a sense of pessimism in the youth about their future.

There is a spatial yardstick that especially affects the intelligentsia. This is the sense which has been growing stronger in the 1980s, that not only are conditions disappointing in Africa, but they are worse than they are in other parts of the world. There are other parts of the world, like Asia, which seem to be doing much better. Africa is faring relatively worse, and again alas, the statistics do bear this out. Since the late 1970s, the

African economic condition has been more dispiriting than that of any other major region.

All this leads to an overwhelming sense that some change has to occur, that something has to happen, and that the instrument to bring about change is democratization. Africans feel that there has to be a remoralization of the moral realm, a reincorporation of civil society. Thus, in his very passionate and stirring presidential address at the American African Studies Association meetings last November, a Zairian scholar, an excellent one of the Marxist persuasion, Nzongola Ntalaja, devoted his address to the theme of democratization. His concluding paragraph ran as follows:

> There is . . . an imperative need for political change. The present crisis cannot be resolved, and development will never be realized under corrupt and authoritarian regimes. . . . We must support the popular struggle for pluralism, democracy, and a more equitable redistribution of wealth. Without a democratic state, without popular participation in decision-making, a people-oriented strategy of development is out of the question.

As a statement, without stipulating what the mix of components of democratization are going to be, that statement commands a remarkable consensus at the present time.

Nearly everyone agrees that elections are going to play a role. Fred Hayward of our department at Wisconsin edited an excellent volume a year ago called *Elections in Independent Africa*, which does demonstrate that even in this authoritarian era, elections have played a more consequential role than many people have thought. Various of the authors present real evidence that elections are valued at different levels of society as an opportunity for expression, rather than simply for their theatrical qualities.

A more difficult, but yet indispensable part of democratization is that—and this is something I picked up in Senegal—alternation of leaders has to take place. A number of single-party systems have been willing to put ministers at risk, but never the leader himself. It doesn't hurt so much for a president to see a few of his ministers go down the drain, even less to see some parliamentarians disappear, because that keeps the clientele circulating. For real democratization to happen, the top office itself has to be up for grabs in some constitutionalized way; the "life-president" formula, where a *coup* is the sole alternative, has to give way to some other kind of formula.

There will be a number of battlegrounds where this issue will be fought out. There will be some rejuvenation of legislatures as an arena of challenge. Certainly the legal realm is another area for democratization; a constitutional state must be an *état de droit.* Local government is yet another arena for democratization, and there are some interesting things going on in this respect in Uganda, Ghana, Nigeria, and some other places. Finally, there needs to be social space for a whole array of associations to spring up. Indeed, new associations are being generated, though in a haphazard way. These associations, which have taken religious, economic, and other forms, have arisen in the face of the relative decay of the credibility and legitimacy of the state. They have developed a new kind of momentum on their own. In the latest issue of *World Politics*, for instance, there is an article by Michael Bratton that makes a strong case for the vitality of this sector, but it needs recognition, support, and incorporation. (I mean "incorporation" in a positive sense, rather than "hegemonical incorporation"; I mean relinkage to the political process.)

We've come a long way in this debate. In 1959 there was a very influential gathering of African intellectuals of that generation at Ibadan. At that time only the Nigerians really wanted competitive parties. There was a general conviction that single-party systems and socialist modes of development strategy could bring a better life to African peoples.

I mentioned that at the level of the nationalist elites themselves, democracy had been a weapon, an arena of combat for the colonial system; it had been a ransom to pay for independence. There were, however, a handful of exceptions. I think it is accurate to say that the commitment to democracy *per se* was not strong amongst that generation of nationalist leaders. However, there are some places where, for peculiar historical circumstances, the colonial state itself left democratic space by accident, as in the "four communes" of Senegal, which go back to 1848.

Later, at the height of the colonial state, colonizers tried to take those liberties back, but they couldn't get away with it. There is a deeply-rooted tradition of democratic competition remaining in coastal Senegal and the Dakar area, for instance, which to some extent has diffused to other parts of the country. Accordingly, it is no accident that Senegal has been a pace-setter in this trend towards restoration of political competition. Freetown, Sierra Leone, was another place where Africans got certain civil rights—some electoral rights, some citizenship type rights—early on, and these went far beyond those accorded to the usual dominated colonial subjects, which was the legal status of most Africans. Those freedoms created something that the British could never have put back in the bottle. In Lagos and its surroundings, similar reforms were made, but these were exceptions to the rule.

That's the good news: There is a consensus in favor of democracy. What's the bad news? There are real limits and perils to this process, which I personally believe is nonetheless indispensable. Africa is being beckoned to democratize its state structures at the same time it faces an extraordinary degree of economic and social distress. The social climate is poisonous in many places. Quite recently there were very serious disorders in Dakar of an ethno-racial sort that had never happened before in the past. Why is it? Because ethnicity or ethno-racial sentiments are stronger now? No, I firmly believe that the poisonous social climate is spilling over into these secondary spheres. The challenge of making the social costs of economic reform compatible with democratization is an enormous one.

A second perilous problem is the importance in most African states, as in states in many other parts of the world (like the Soviet Union for example), of cultural pluralism. That problem hasn't gone away, and is not going to go away; it is always going to be a part of the political environment in changing forms. Even in Great Britain, the land of Westminster and home of competitive democracy, democratic rule in Ulster is always a sham, because there will always remain a Protestant majority there. There is a fundamental flaw in the dynamic of democracy when you have polarized, bipolar societies like Northern Ireland. That kind of polarization doesn't really operate in Senegal, these recent tragedies notwithstanding.

There are places in Africa where it does operate, however, such as the Sudan. Sudan does at this moment have an elected government, but that very elected government is incapable of taking the decisions that would permit a solution to the Sudan crisis, which are to get rid of the "September laws." There is a simple solution available. A dissident movement, the SPLA, does not insist on breaking up the state, but it does insist that Christian Sudanese not be subjected to a rigorous, integralist, Islamic state, since they are not part of that culture. Yet the National Islamic Front has enough electoral weight so that it is very difficult to get around them.

Finally, there is the peril of over advertising democracy as a remedy for Africa's travails. Democracy is in certain respects an end, no doubt, but it is to my mind perhaps more importantly a means towards salvaging the African state by reconnecting it to civil society. Even that reconnection, in and of itself, however necessary and indispensable it is, only solves one aspect of the crisis confronting the African state. There are many other vicious cycles within which the contemporary African state is enclosed and democracy in and of itself, whatever form it might take, will not provide a complete response. Rather, it can only be a means towards the search for such an answer.

QUESTION: I would like to ask you something about the meaning of the word "democracy." I can understand that there are various perceptions and interpretations of it, but the definition of democracy seems to require no debate. It comes from the Greek root meaning "people," and it means what it says in our Constitution, "Of the people, by the people, for the people." My own definition is very simple: A system in which the people choose their leaders, or it is rule of the people. I don't know how you can get away from that.

Secondly, I am concerned that you speak of constitutionalism as if it were a form of government. My understanding is that the constitution merely documents the form of government that a state has. It isn't in itself a form of government; it just pins it down so that everybody knows what it is. Perhaps you could clarify your use of these simple concepts, which seemed so complicated in your talk.

PROFESSOR YOUNG: Well, they are simple concepts in a sense; that's true. When I am teaching Political Science 101, I rely upon a definition similar to the one that you just proposed, which goes back to the etymology of the term. When you try to take that concept and apply it to Zaire, for instance, a whole host of secondary questions arise as we try to translate an idea into an actual form of government. In the same sense, those who have been constitution-drafters in many parts of the world have come to many different formulas for putting that idea into practice. The British understanding, which includes parliamentary supremacy, the unwritten constitution, etc., is very different from our own. There is a fundamental divide between the Anglo-American state, a relatively modest state on the historical scale, and the continental, Bonapartist type state that was a model for the construction of many other states.

West Germany and Japan, whose present constitutions were drafted partly by outsiders with the very specific idea of preventing a return of aggressive, militaristic forces that had in the past rendered those countries rogue elephants on the world scene, are other constitutional variants. Thus I think that there remain, even if we agree on a core notion of what democracy is, many challenges as to how it can be adapted.

I think you have described something we know as "the constitution." I believe there is a system of rule called constitutionalism, and that is a term that does exist within the discipline. Carl Frederich, one of the authors of the West German Constitution, had a weighty tome on the subject that influenced many of us in graduate school long ago.

Constitutionalism, in the way I've used the term, means a form of rule in which the constitution does authoritatively and definitively shape and guide the ongoing operation of the polity. It is a system where there are rules of the game, and these rules do constitute a kind of compact between state and citizenry which assures the citizenry that the state is accountable, responsive in some sense to their will.

QUESTION: Is it perhaps more likely that those countries will, in the course of time, develop a sort of custom or practice that guides the way government leaders are selected? Is something like the British concept of traditional common law constitution possible? Rather than having some group of lawyers from New York or Charlottesville write down a constitution, *their* "constitution" evolved from practice. From your discussion, it occurs to me that it may be a very long time before they will have things like our presidential primaries and general elections of the top ruler. In fact, it may not even be a good idea.

PROFESSOR YOUNG: Firstly, with respect to the role that organic growth plays in constitutional forms, surely that will have an important part. There is a whole school of thought, which I think has important validity, that in fact many (though not all), precolonial African states were much more democratic than the colonial states. Even if they had monarchical forms of some sort, there were mechanisms by which kings were made accountable to notables. There were ways in which the subjects as a whole could exercise some constraint upon the rulers, and there was a kind of democratic process. It would go much too far to say that this was universal among precolonial African states, but there were certainly a substantial number. This was above all the case for those that were long-established where this kind of custom had grown up. The ones that didn't correspond to this conception were the ones which there were recent military conquests, or they were *jihad* states where rule was established simply by force. In these states no such restraints had emerged.

I agree, of course, that organic growth must be a necessary part of the process. I think you've read me rightly if you have inferred from this analysis that there is a dynamic of democratization which I believe is in action; I believe that it is happening even if it is not going to occur overnight. It will be an evolution, a development over time which will doubtless have its retreats as well as forward movements. Custom is very definitely an important part. To go back to the democratic, or apparently democratic, systems established at the end of the colonial period, a fatal flaw in them was that they had, with few exceptions that I noted, no tradition to back them. They were suddenly injected into the international system overnight, and they were vulnerable; they were fragile.

QUESTION: While I certainly have enjoyed your presentation, I am unfortunately a bit more skeptical than you about this trend of democratization that you think is at work. Consider, for instance, the continuing or indeed increasing repression in African states like Malawi, Kenya, South Africa, Angola, Zaire, or say, Swaziland. Could you illustrate for me how this trend has affected these states?

PROFESSOR YOUNG: Well, there are fifty-one, going on fifty-two states in Africa, and the trend is hardly universal. I think that in a couple of those cases an argument can be made that democratic ideas are at work in a limited way, even when the states still seem very repressive. In South Africa, for instance, democratic ideas are little by little weighing more heavily upon that system. By that I mean that the excluded portions of the population, as they gather social consciousness and strength, are making the contradictions of South Africa's system of democracy for whites and repression for others more visible.

Likewise, in the other one-party states that you mentioned, the pressures on the current regimes are becoming greater. Even if the process of political change appears to be slow, or even retrograde, in those states, it is becoming clear that their present model of political organization will not work. There is going to have to be an adjustment, and that adjustment is going to have to take account, one way or another, of other political forces in these countries. How that is going to work out, who will take part, and what visible personalities it will include or will not include are all things that only the future will tell. Still, I think that a loosened up political formula will emerge from that process.

Zaire might seem to be the toughest case because the Mobutu regime is so repressive, and yet it is an interesting case in that the instant that a little latitude is given there, it is amazing what people will do. There was a period of time in the late 1970s when, as a condition for aid, certain political reforms were demanded by outside forces; that is, in order to have the continuing support of the U.S. and other Western and international financial agencies, there was going to have to be some loosening of the political system. Zaire was in critical need of aid for a bailout at the time. In keeping with the political conditionality, the parliament was given some opportunity for a period of time to interpolate ministers. At the moment they got that opportunity, they went after them. A commission of parliamentarians went down to the Zaire's Central Bank and demanded to see the vouchers of Mobutu's withdrawals. It was those vouchers, the documentation that parliamentary commission obtained, which Nguza Karl-I-Bond then gave to an American congressional committee. The documents showed something like $150 million of unauthorized withdrawals of foreign exchange over a short period of time by Mobutu and his immediate family. When that sort of thing started happening, of course, Mobutu put an end to it. There was no more interpellation of ministers, and no more trips to the Central Bank, but nonetheless it showed what will happen when a tiny opportunity is available.

Just recently one of my successors as dean of the faculty at the University of Lubumbashi gave his account of the kinds of things that are now happening in Zaire's Parliament, and suggests that there is some recycling of that late 1970s experience. Even in Zaire, then, there are some prospects for an opening of the system and more scrutiny of corruption.

Regarding Kenya, you are quite correct in what you didn't say, but implied. It is true that the recent trend has been towards a tightening of that system, that the trend towards democracy hasn't really occurred yet. Still, I do think that over time President arap Moi is going to find himself increasingly on the defensive. Kenya is really under attack by the human rights groups, which was not the case until very recently. It begins to be hard to sell the case for Kenyan aid in Congress, whereas ten years ago Kenya was the great miracle story. There is definitely a set of pressures at work that may have some effect over time. Certainly among the Kenyan intelligentsia, there is an aspiration for change in the system such as was conveyed by the Anyang' Nyong'o quotation that I read.

QUESTION: My question has to do with literacy. There are many aspects of democracy such as you described at the beginning, which we should look for as signs of the acceptance of Western democratic principles. As you mentioned in an answer to another question, though, there was a certain kind of African democracy that existed by consensus in certain African kingdoms in the precolonial era. There were councils of elders, for instance, that served as democratic links between the masses and the village chiefs. That was something that illiterate people could understand. The authoritarianism of the colonial state was something that people were forced to understand.

The examples that you cited which were more successful cases of democratic activity in the way that we understand it had higher literacy in common. Lagos, the "fout communes of Senegal" and Freetown were areas where literacy was at a more advanced state than in many of the other areas that we have discussed. So I would like to know if you think that literacy and education in the Western sense would be a prerequisite for the extension of democracy as we know it, and if so, what about a case like Ivory Coast where you have increasing levels of educated young people coming out of school?

PROFESSOR YOUNG: Well, elitists always advance an argument, which replicates the arguments of colonial authorities, as to why voting, insofar as it exists at all, should be restricted to very small numbers of people. Until the very end of the colonial period, this was supposed to be the quick path to acquiring any kind of representative institutions at all. The access to the print media that literacy gives the citizen is an important factor. However, I wouldn't say that it is an absolute prerequisite to the kind of political sophistication that is required for meaningful participation.

Fred Hayward did some very interesting surveys on levels of political information in rural Ghana in the 1970s. Interviewing local inhabitants—I don't recollect the fraction of illiterate respondents picked up in the survey, but it would have been substantial—he found a remarkably high level of political information. Political information does diffuse. It diffuses much less through newspapers than through the taxi buses that leave the capitol every morning and spread out to the four corners of the country with their passengers, carrying along the latest news from the capitol. Likewise radio, since the transistor revolution, is in many respects a more potent medium than the written word.

Newspapers don't frankly make very inspirational reading in most countries, because they are essentially government information office publications. Therefore, they have long, tedious official communiques about this, that and the other thing. You can't really find out what is going on just by reading the newspapers; you have to have other channels of information that don't necessarily rely upon literacy for access.

I do think, of course, the more literacy there is, the better. I don't think that it is indispensable to opening up political systems to greater degrees of participation. If people in Zaire are cynical about the state, it is not because some of them can't read, but because they know very well how the state works. They have a shrewd, sophisticated understanding of what politics is, who gets what, when and how, and what's going on, and they don't like it. Anything that helps them, whether it is local associations, local governments, competitive elections, or whatever it is that gives them more and forces government to be more accountable to them, is going to be helpful.

I didn't answer the question about primary elections, or about exactly what electoral form should be adopted. In fact, primary elections have been fairly widely used within the single-party system. Indeed, Mobutu himself made very shrewd use of this weapon, saying that there could be an unlimited number of contestants for the election as long as they were in his party. This policy generated ten or fifteen candidates per seat, greatly fragmenting factions that might have opposed Mobutu. Among other things, it eliminated ethnic blocs as a factor because there were too many people for ethnic blocs to form in the election. It also meant, of course, that no shadowy, anti-regime coalitions could form. Tanzania pioneered this primary formula within the single-party framework in 1965.

Speaking of Tanzania, there are interesting and intriguing rumors that Nyerere himself would like to come back to power, which would add a new dimension to politics within the single party. I don't know if this is true, but he is reportedly disappointed with the direction that his successor has taken. The rumors have it that he may re-assert himself at the Party Congress in 1990 prior to the next presidential elections. Other people cast doubt on that rumor. I don't know how much there is to it, but if it were to transpire, then you would see a very interesting competition grow up at the Party Congress. Whatever the outcome, it might well form part of this process of democratization that we are talking about.

QUESTION: I have two questions, both of which relate to your argument here today that democratization is the dominant idea for the future.

First, what is the locus for this new fascination with democracy? It certainly is not popular among African statesmen who actually hold power right now. They've been doing everything they can to suppress opposition and to forestall change. Nor is there a consensus among the peasantry in favor of democracy. I certainly don't see any consensus among the leadership.

Secondly, I'd like to ask a specific question about Ethiopia. You argued in your talk that much of Africa's current authoritarianism could be traced back to the legacy of colonial rule. Yet Ethiopia was never really colonized by Europeans, and it has one of the most repressive governments, next to South Africa, on the continent. How do you account for that?

PROFESSOR YOUNG: I've always said that it is up to the intelligentsia, the intellectuals to solidify this consensus for change. The people who are now in power and want to stay there, of course, don't necessarily share this consensus on the therapeutic value of democracy. When the

Senegalese elections ran into trouble, and there was a certain degree of violence, who was the first person to issue a press release but Omar Bongo of Gabon. He said something to the effect, "See, this shows that a single-party system is the only realistic formula for Africa." And then Mobutu and others in power made similar kinds of statements. I don't include in this consensus incumbent rulers in the same way.

Looking at this process as it is occurring elsewhere, rulers want both to reform their societies and to keep power. For instance, I don't think Gorbachev wants to dismantle Communist Party rule in the Soviet Union. Rather, he wants to open the system up some to use those changes as an instrument for fulfilling his vision of some economic reorganization *without* abandoning the system. Fortunately, these things take on a life of their own; they gather their own momentum. And those in power who have one aspiration for what a little reform may do, may not be able to control the channels into which it eventually flows.

I do want to come back to this point about the need for pluralism and participation. I am struck by things such as Nzongola's presidential speech where he develops those themes; it is quite significant. There have been a whole series of books by African intellectuals on the issue of democracy in the last two or three years. There are some who don't share this conviction, but the great majority of them cutting across the ideological spectrum do. That, to my mind, is an important transformation and is in itself generating pressures for further movement.

Your second question dealt with the connection of authoritarianism and the colonial state. There is a wonderful article by Michael Crowder in *African Affairs* in 1987 entitled, "Whose Dream Was it Anyway?" This article takes issue with the condemnation of the African state for being corrupt, dictatorial, authoritarian, etc., as one often sees reported. It nicely traces every one of these traits back to the colonial state itself. The colonial state came into being in Africa in very special circumstances in which it was obliged rapidly to consolidate its domination or hegemony and at the same time required by metropolitan parliaments to do so with little expenditure from metropolitan treasuries. Furthermore, in most of Africa there was no revenue source. So how do you solve that problem? You have to institutionalize rule, and you have to somehow make the population pay for it.

Thus, the logic and behavior of the structuring of the colonial state to an extraordinary degree in its early years revolved around the question of organizing African labor. African labor had to be made to generate a revenue flow for the colonial state, either through forced cultivation of crops that could be taxed at the point of their export or through direct head taxation, which provided, until the 1930s, the bulk of the revenue for the colonial state. Also, forced recruitment for labor in European enterprises of different sorts provided revenues from the taxes on those products. This revenue-gathering led in turn to a kind of superstructure of rule based on authoritarianism. It's true that it became less harsh in its later years than in the earlier ones, but still it had a kind of logic that could only repose upon a whole battery of arbitrary legislation.

The British, for instance, had different kinds of detention ordinances and other master and servant ordinances and so forth that vested a kind of arbitrary power in the state. The state then used its power to seize direction of the economy for its own survival. African colonial rule was really different from India, for example. There was a land record; the British didn't need to do the same things to India that they did in Kenya or Uganda. Consequently, I believe that to understand why India, with the exception of the brief period of the emergency, retained constitutional forms while Africa did not, you have to look at the differences in the operation and logic of the colonial state.

QUESTION: How do you account for Ethiopia's authoritarianism, if colonialism is to blame?

PROFESSOR YOUNG: Well, Ethiopia was an unusual kind of state in the nature of its social structure. It is one of the only African states where, even debatably, you can use the term "feudalism" to describe it. Most of Africa didn't have that kind of economic structure. Ethiopia did have a revenue flow, that's true, but still it was quite precarious until Haile Selassie modernized the state. I did not intend to make the argument that the colonial state provided *all* the explanation or that only in cases where you've had a colonial state like the African one do you get autocratic outcomes. There are evidently many countries in the world that have developed autocratic forms without the "benefit" of a colonial state.

QUESTION: Do you observe any differences in the second generation of African leaders in comparison with the first generation in terms of their willingness to tolerate opposition, their economic policies, etc.? Secondly, how does the "economy of affection" that is being discussed in the contemporary literature on Africa fit in with your democratization thesis?

PROFESSOR YOUNG: Well, those are both very interesting questions. I still reserve judgment on some of the second generation of leaders, like Jerry Rawlings in Ghana. I don't know how that's all going to work itself out. I do think that Rawlings' style of political management is different from that of Acheampong or of Nkrumah. He is trying to contend forcefully with a complex of political forces, but not in ways that are simply coercive; nor are his methods simply the kind of patrimonial management that we've seen in so many places. Oddly enough, Ghana is the prize pupil of the international financial agencies, the IMF and World Bank, in terms of the structural adjustment it has applied. Ghana, of course, was an extreme case in terms of the deterioration of its economy; there were few states that were in such wretched condition by the low point of African economies in 1983. It certainly has come back some since that time. Because of its prize-pupil standing, it has gotten unusually high levels of foreign assistance. It is true, too, that there are competent people, good people in that second generation in Ghana. Honestly, I can't easily sort out in my own mind what is the combination of policies pursued, the aid level received, the political formulas used, and the quality of the people who are running that whole process, that have made Ghana relatively successful.

If you talk about arap Moi or Samuel Doe as second generation people, they recall to mind the first generation; they are the first generation two times over!

QUESTION: Related to that question, could you identify some of the African students among your contacts who studied abroad in the 1960s, particularly those who studied at Patrice Lumumba University and Law School in Moscow? I believe it was during the 1960s that the African authorities quipped that the students who went to Paris came home communists, and the ones who went to Moscow came back capitalists. Do you have any insights into how study abroad has affected the African intelligentsia?

PROFESSOR YOUNG: There is a little bit of truth to that. One of the notable things that has happened is that the size and scale of the African intelligentsia is vastly greater than it was in the 1950s. To use this Zairian case again, although it was not true, as it was widely said, that there were only sixteen university students—there were quite a few more than that as we count them—the underlying point that they were very few in relation to the size of the country was true. Thus, it was possible to argue, as foundations and many other people used to believe, that all Zaire needed was some educated people and everything would be fine. Today, however, Zaire has lots of educated people, lots of very skilled people, and things are perhaps worse than ever, so it's not a human resource issue in Zaire at all now. Indeed, I think that comment can be applied to most African states; most states are now endowed with an infrastructure of skilled people, except for in some highly technical kinds of fields. There is not really a shortage of very talented and able people.

Does it make a difference where they studied? Well, I think less and less so. Certainly a place like Charlottesville has its own intellectual milieu, and it has, I'm sure, some impact on those students who study here, both in terms of what they absorb and what they reject or criticize. This rejection is what has happened with the capitalists coming back from Moscow. It's not that they absorbed nothing in Moscow, but that there has been both an absorption and a rejection process interacting with each other in their exposure to this culture.

Something else that's important, which is a much less happy trend, is the loss of elites to the West. Ethiopia, for example, has lost enormous numbers of talented people. It first lost a whole generation at the time of the Italian occupation; that was one generation that went. Later some left under Emperor Selassie, though not all that many. Since 1974 there has been a big exodus of Ethiopians, and our country has been the beneficiary of that. We've received a lot of talented people, but it is a tragedy for Ethiopia that so many people have been driven out of the country because they feel that they cannot work there. Then ten to twenty years go by, that exiled generation acquires families, their children go to schools in their country of adoption, and it becomes difficult to go back, even if they want to.

For example, Guinea is a country that has had a lot of exiles, including many very good ones. After Sekou finally passed away and a new regime came in, they went back to test the waters. By then they found that people didn't want them because the people were thinking, "We stayed here all these years and suffered and you were in Paris or Los Angeles, living in comfort, getting good salaries and so forth. Now you want to come back and take the good jobs. No, sir." Over a period of time the hemorrhage becomes permanent and the exiles can't go back. Thus there has been, as a consequence of the nature of many African states, a substantial loss of highly skilled persons that Africa could ill afford.

QUESTION: You have acknowledged that the economic condition of African countries is worsening regardless of the political changes. How do you account for that? Secondly, you say that there is a crisis and a consensus for change in almost every country. Do you think that consensus for change was brought on by worsening economic conditions or was it due to political repression?

PROFESSOR YOUNG: I think it is both political and economic, don't you? I think it is both of those things, but in different ways in different countries. There are some countries that are not particularly repressive. Senegal is not particularly repressive, while Zaire definitely is. Thus in Zaire people are reacting both to a sense of a continuing economic decline and to the perpetual political repression.

This becomes so deeply built into the popular consciousness that people are feeling ever more hopeless. Every time I see one of my friends in Zaire and ask, "How are things going? Are things getting any better economically?" they reply, "No, no; we are getting worse." People are so strongly convinced that things are getting worse, in fact, that I think they would have to get better for a long time before anybody perceived that there was a change in the situation.

At the same time they are very disaffected from the political system. Even people at the very top echelons of the regime are cynical. One's conversation with Zairian colleagues always begins with a series of lamentations about the nature of the regime. If there is a group that has come together, people always have a collection of anecdotes. One will say, "Have you heard what Mobutu just did?" and the next person will reply, "Oh, that's nothing; I've got an even better story than that." Thus both political and economic disaffection go together.

In Senegal, by contrast, it is really the economic and social situation that is the driving force behind the sentiment for change. In that sense Senegal may be representative of the less repressive African states.

NARRATOR: I know we all wish that we could go on for another hour or two because Crawford Young has introduced us to such intriguing ideas. We are terribly grateful to him for coming, especially with his busy schedule, and we look forward to future visits. I certainly learned a lot, as I am sure we all did.